Pier Francesco Listri

ROME and the
VATICAN CITY
VENICE
FLORENCE
NAPLES

ATS Italia Editrice – Kina Italia/Eurografica – Editrice Giusti

VENICE

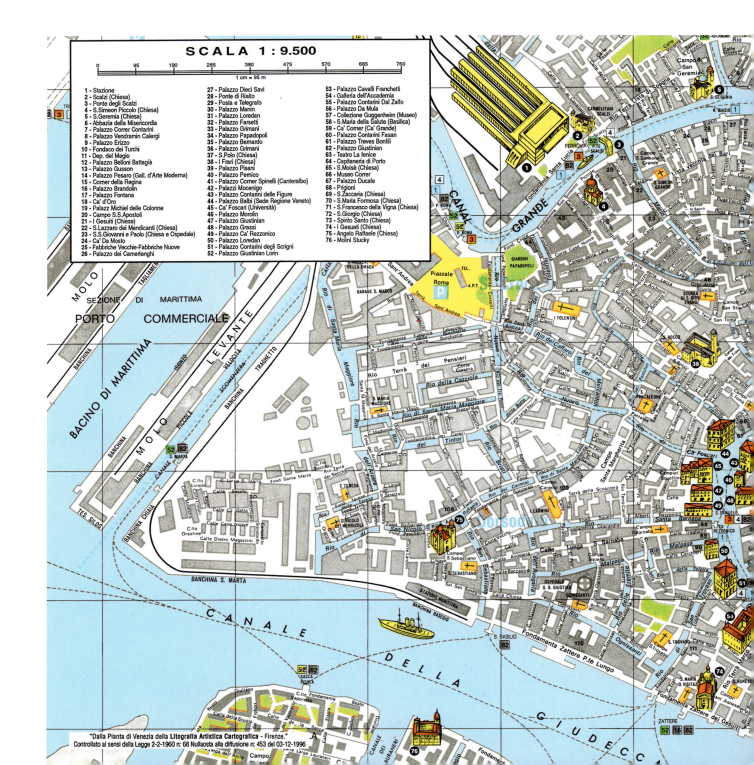

SCALA 1 : 9.500

0 95 190 285 380 475 570 665 760
1 cm = 95 m

1 - Stazione
2 - Scalzi (Chiesa)
3 - Ponte degli Scalzi
4 - S.Simeon Piccolo (Chiesa)
5 - S.Geremia (Chiesa)
6 - Abbazia della Misericordia
7 - Palazzo Correr Contarini
8 - Palazzo Vendramin Calergi
9 - Palazzo Erizzo
10 - Fondaco dei Turchi
11 - Dep. del Megio
12 - Palazzo Belloni Battagià
13 - Palazzo Gusson
14 - Corner della Regina
15 - Palazzo Pesaro (Gall. d'Arte Moderna)
16 - Palazzo Brandolin
17 - Palazzo Fontana
18 - Ca' d'Oro
19 - Palazz Michiel delle Colonne
20 - Campo S.S.Apostoli
21 - I Gesuiti (Chiesa)
22 - S.Lazzaro dei Mendicanti (Chiesa)
23 - S.S.Giovanni e Paolo (Chiesa e Ospedale)
24 - Ca' Da Mosto
25 - Fabbriche Vecchie-Fabbriche Nuove
26 - Palazzo dei Camerlenghi

27 - Palazzo Dieci Savi
28 - Ponte di Rialto
29 - Posta e Telegrafo
30 - Palazzo Manin
31 - Palazzo Loredan
32 - Palazzo Farsetti
33 - Palazzo Grimani
34 - Palazzo Papadopoli
35 - Palazzo Bernardo
36 - Palazzo Grimani
37 - S.Polo (Chiesa)
38 - I Frari (Chiesa)
39 - Palazzo Pisani
40 - Palazzo Pemico
41 - Palazzo Corner Spinelli (Canteralbo)
42 - Palazzi Mocenigo
43 - Palazzo Contarini delle Figure
44 - Palazzo Balbi (Sede Regione Veneto)
45 - Ca' Foscari (Università)
46 - Palazzo Morolin
47 - Palazzo Giustinian
48 - Palazzo Grassi
49 - Palazzo Ca' Rezzonico
50 - Palazzo Loredan
51 - Palazzo Contarini degli Scrigni
52 - Palazzo Giustinian Lorin

53 - Palazzo Cavalli Franchetti
54 - Galleria dell'Accademia
55 - Palazzo Contarini Dal Zalfo
56 - Palazzo Da Mula
57 - Collezione Guggenheim (Museo)
58 - S.Maria della Salute (Basilica)
59 - Ca' Corner (Ca' Grande)
60 - Palazzo Contarini Fasan
61 - Palazzo Treves Bonfili
62 - Palazzo Giustinian
63 - Teatro La fenice
64 - Capitaneria di Porto
65 - S.Moisè (Chiesa)
66 - Museo Correr
67 - Palazzo Ducale
68 - Prigioni
69 - S.Zaccaria (Chiesa)
70 - S.Maria Formosa (Chiesa)
71 - S.Francesco della Vigna (Chiesa)
72 - S.Giorgio (Chiesa)
73 - Spirito Santo (Chiesa)
74 - I Gesuati (Chiesa)
75 - Angelo Raffaele (Chiesa)
76 - Molini Stucky

"Dalla Pianta di Venezia della Litografia Artistica Cartografica - Firenze."
Controllato ai sensi della Legge 2-2-1960 n: 68 Nullaosta alla diffusione n: 453 del 03-12-1996

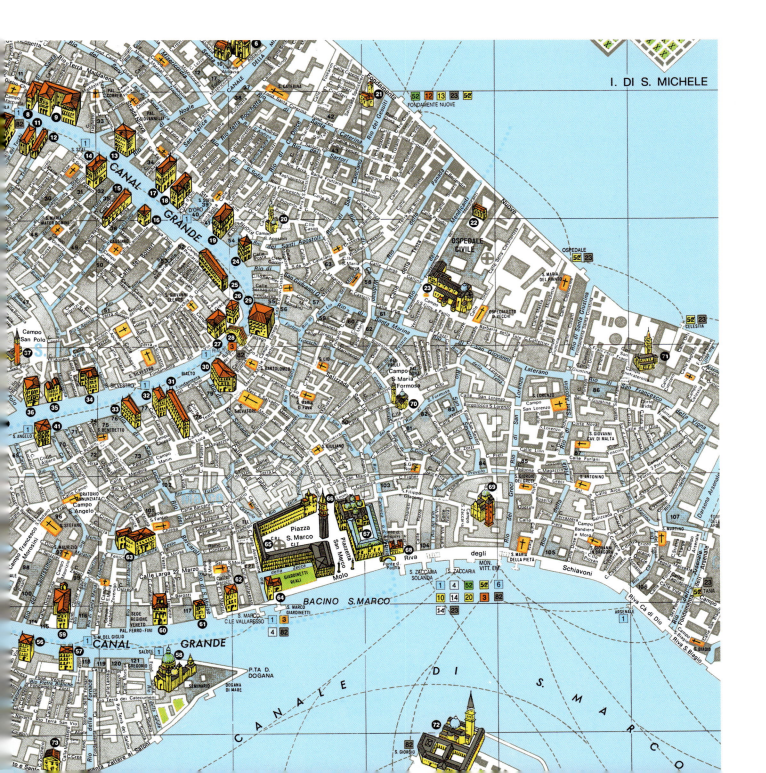

historical background

Built on a hundred and twenty little islands, linked to the mainland by four hundred bridges, Venice is unique. And not only from an architectural point of view: fifteen centuries of history makes her fascinating. Venice was a maritime republic and invented a unique political system (the Dogate) with elements of both a republic and a monarchy that was to last a thousand years. She acquired political and commercial power that stretched beyond the Mediterranean as far as Asia (Marco Polo, for instance, got as far as China in 1271). Thanks to its swift galleys, Venice was queen of the seas, and a bridge between Eastern and Western culture (St. Mark's is a basilica with a Byzantine dome, but dedicated to a Roman saint).

Today, in spite of its visible and probably inevitable decadence (the serious threat of the high tides, the erosion of the palaces, the exodus of the population from the city), Venice keeps intact, perhaps as no other city in the world, the impression of something never to be repeated, of a high cultural level sprung from a precarious and fleeting encounter between the sea and history.

It is believed that Venice was originally founded when the neighbouring inhabitants of Aquileia, Monselice and Altino, fled the Hun barbarians and found refuge on the islets of the lagoon. And so was born the solitary appendix of a Roman Byzantine province. The flourishing port of Torcello was founded here and already by the 5th century was a bishopric.

The Duke (Doge) slowly acquired autonomy from the Emperor which enabled Orso Ipati, the first Doge, to inaugurate a political system that was to last a thousand years. The ties with the Byzantine emperor were excellent to begin with, but later degenerated. In 822 AD the body of St. Mark, a Roman saint, was brought from Alexandria (Egypt) to Venice. Thus it came about that, in spite of her origins and her ties with Byzantium, Venice took on the identity of a Western and Christian city. In 829 AD the Ducal Chapel, that is the Basilica of St. Mark's, was built next to the Doges' Palace in what is now St. Mark's Square. The style was Eastern, yet dedicated to a Roman saint. From now on the Lion became the symbol of the Venetian Republic.

Meanwhile the Venetian galleys conquered the Adriatic and Mediterranean seas, pushing towards the East. Now become a maritime republic together with Pisa, Amalfi and Genoa, by the 11th century Venice was a power to be reckoned with. She gave her support to the Crusaders. The Venetians established important maritime trading stations, enjoyed trading privileges with countries as farflung as Egypt and reached as far as Asia (thanks to Marco Polo). The galleys took cargoes of wool, silk, timber and metals, and brought back for the European markets spices, wheat, silk and precious stones.

The first real political and commercial opponent was Genoa, whose maritime interests conflicted with those of Venice. Soon, however, another enemy loomed on the horizon: the Ottomans. Turks and Islam became the great ever-present enemies.

However, there were also enemies on the mainland: the increasingly powerful Visconti family in Milan became a constant source of trouble. Venice, meanwhile, had created a balanced, and in its way unique method of governing the Republic.

The Doge was the head of the state, its supreme ruler. But to avoid any form of monarchical absolutism, Venice created a series of counterweights to this power: the great Council, the Council of Ten etc. These were composed chiefly of nobles and prominent merchants. Venice fought on many fronts in the 13th century: an outbreak of the plague reduced the population by half; Genoa rivalled its maritime power, and the Ottomans became an even greater threat (in many battles Venice was defeated by the Turks).

In the 15th century Venice was flourishing. The Republic conquered Cyprus and on the mainland: Padua, Vicenza, Verona and later Friuli. Her increasing power forced France and the Pope to form the League of Cambrai against her. The Pope was later to break this alliance in favour of one with Venice.

Venice also flourished culturally. The Renaissance spread from Florence to Venice thanks to the art of Leon Battista Alberti, Donatello and their followers such as Pietro Lombardo and Mauro Coducci. The harmony and rationalism of the Renaissance prompted new architectural feats in Venice: the Scuola di San Giovanni Evangelista, Scuola di San Marco, Palazzo Vendramin, Palazzo Corner Spinelli and Santa Maria dei Miracoli. In the early 16th century Sansovino built the Marcian Library in St. Mark's Square. Inside and around these works of architecture great painters like Titian, Tintoretto, Giorgione and Jacopo

da Bassano painted their masterpieces, using Florentine "line" and drawing with Venetian "colour".
Despite the decline of political power in Venice in the 17th century (the loss of Cyprus and maritime control, as well as severe epidemics of the plague), her artistic splendour remained intact and were built: the Chiesa della Salute, the beautiful Rezzonico and Pesaro palaces on the Grand Canal by Longhena, the Seminario and the Dogana.

From an artistic point of view, the 18th century is one of the greatest periods in Venetian history.

In painting great names are: Tiepolo and the "vedutisti" Longhi, Canaletto and Guardi (owing to whom we now have a precise and enchanting record of 18th century Venetian society). In architecture memorable are: Palazzo Grassi, Palazzo Pisani, the Churches of San Stae and of the Gesuati, and the Fenice theatre (recently burnt to the ground) where the immortal works of Benedetto Marcello, Vivaldi and Boccherini, all Venetians, were performed.

These artistic splendours contrast with a rapid political and economic decline which paradoxically stems from the famous Venetian victory at Lepanto (1571). Lepanto was the decisive and final battle between Venice and the Ottoman Empire; secure in the alliance of the Holy League (made up of Spain under Philip II and Pope Pius V), Venice put to sea two hundred galleys (with more firing power than the two hundred and sixty Turkish ships).

The Venetians defeated the Turks, who lost thirty thousand lives during this terrible battle. Nevertheless the power of Venice was doomed and slowly declined: Cyprus was lost, the Turks again started to close in from the East and eventually Venice was vanquished by the Napoleonic troops. By the treaty of Campo Formio (1797) Venice was ceded to Austria by Napoleon in a move which proved an advantage to himself. The ensuing unhappy period in the city's history was broken only by the anti-Austrian uprising of 1848 which led to the formation of a short-lived republic. However, in 1849 Austria reoccupied the city. By public consent, Venice was annexed to Italy in 1866.

The end of the 19th century, and the beginning of the 20th, saw a cultural revival in Venice. The port was reorganised and an attempt was made to create industries in Mestre. The Biennale Internazionale d'Arte and the Film Festival were instituted and tourism slowly started flourishing.

In spite of the special law of 1973, the fate of Venice appears uncertain and precarious: there is a significant exodus from the city centre, water erosion and high tides threaten the palaces and the foundations – the very structure of the city. Industry is not progressing; it seems as if the service sector is the only one holding the key to the city's future. Tourism holds good and is ever increasing, because the spell of Venice is not yet spent.

St. Mark's Square

As a meeting-place, theatre and court of honour, St. Mark's Square has always been the heart of Venice. Here all relevant symbols are gathered together: the religious symbol (in the form of the Basilica), political power (the Doges' Palace), justice (the Procuratie) and culture (the Marcian Library).

Above all, there are the fourteen winged lions along the square, guardians of Venetian power that came from the sea. St. Mark's Square is the only square in Venice called a "piazza"; the others are called "campi". Processions, cortèges, ceremonies, celebrations, plays, executions... the square has witnessed them all. Among the better known processions still taking place are: the procession of Corpus Domini at the beginning of June and the investiture of the "Great Captain of the Sea". During carnival time, St. Mark's Square became a gigantic stage for bull races, wheelbarrow races, clowns, people in fancy dress, men on stilts and exotic animals. All the past grandeur is no longer visible, but every stone still reflects, as Le Corbusier said, "all the techniques and all the materials". Although the eye is immediately drawn to the opulence of the Basilica, you should first look at all the signs of Venetian history which surround it. Around 800 AD the square was divided in two by the Rio Batario: in 1100 this canal was built-over and so this square was made. The Procuratie Vecchie (the Old Procuratie) were built, consisting only of one floor. At the beginning of 1000 AD the Doges' Palace was still a fortified castle and the present Bell Tower a watch tower over the sea.

The square was first paved with bricks in a herringbone pattern in 1200 AD; the present pavement dates from the 18th century. Between the 14th and 15th centuries, the Basilica assumed

a pointed Gothic look as was then the fashion. And the Doges' Palace was also restructured in the same style but with Islamic touches. At the beginning of the 16th century the famous Clock Tower was built by the brothers Carlo and Paolo Rainieri. According to legend they were blinded so that they could never build elsewhere such a magnificent and perfect building. The clock not only shows the time but also the lunar phases and the Zodiac. It was invaluable to sailors as it indicated the tides and all information necessary to put to sea. In the same period the Procuratie Vecchie, destroyed by fire, assumed their present appearance. In mid-century Sansovino, the Republic's chief architect, remodelled the square and built the Zecca and the Marcian Library. At the end of the 16th century Scamozzi built the Procuratie Nuove (the New Procuratie) completed half a century later by Longhena. The Napoleonic Wing was added in the 19th century at the wish of the Emperor. The square was then complete. We will visit it together.

The two columns with the statues of St. Theodore and of the winged lion

From the procuratie to the Marcian Library

The Bell Tower is 97 metres high. If you climb to the top, you will enjoy a splendid view of the city and the lagoons. In July 1902 the tower suddenly collapsed, but was rebuilt on the same spot exactly as it had been.

On the opposite side of the square stands the Clock Tower at the entrance of the Mercerie, the busiest thoroughfare in the city.

The building is 15th century, the side wings and the terrace are of a later date. In the middle is the Clock, over it the Lion of St. Mark and at the top the famous "Moors" who, at stated hours, by a series of complicated devices, ring the big Bell. The Marcian Library is today one of the most important in Italy, consisting as it does of a million books, superb nautical maps and miniatures, among which the well-known Grimani Breviary. The latter was named after the 16th century cardinal and theologian and is a Flemish work of the 15th and 16th centuries. The Marcian Library originated with the bequest of Francesco Petrarca's personal library. This was later added to by the precious library of the Humanist cardinal Bessarione. The building, dating from the middle of the 16th century and designed by Sansovino, merges the classic and Venetian styles, and stands out because of its Doric arcades, the long line of windows and its overhanging terrace. Inside there are important examples of Venetian Mannerist painting: on the ceiling of the hall there is Titian's Wisdom, and works of Veronese. Do not miss a visit to the Zecca, another work of Sansovino which is now part of the Library. Here once were minted silver ducats, golden "scudi", and "oselle" (coins used throughout the world in the heyday of the Republic).

The big clock under the Lion of St. Mark

Sansovino's Loggia

In the dense throng of tourists, almost as numerous as the pigeons, do not miss the three "Pili", other relics of the glory that once was Venice. These ancient masts were already placed in the square by the end of the 15th century. Following an old tradition, on feast days the gold and red standards of the Republic are raised on the masts and placed in front of the portals of the Basilica. At the back of the "piazzetta" (little square) stand two Eastern Columns in red and grey granite. There was a third one but it sank into the sea. On the top of one is a statue of St. Theodore (called "Todaro" in Venice), one time patron saint of the city; on the other a statue of St. Mark defeating the dragon as well as a winged lion, weighing three tons, facing the sea.

St. Mark's Basilica

St. Mark's is almost a thousand years old. It is one of the most magnificent and important of Christian churches. Imposing and distinctive – with five hundred columns and four thousand square metres of mosaics – it at once embodies a wonderful balance between many overlapping styles, Byzantine, Gothic, Eastern, and the constant willingness of Venice to remain open to Eastern influence. The latter was in fact the dominating influence at this time. The history of the Basilica goes back to the year 832 AD when the Venetians built a church to honour St. Mark's remains stolen from the Mohammedans of Alexandria (Egypt). St. Mark became the patron saint of the city replacing St. Theodore (called "Todaro" in Venice), thus shaking off Byzantium power. It did not become the Cathedral of Venice until 1807. During a popular uprising shortly before 1000 AD, the Doges' Palace was set on fire; the flames reached the neighbouring church that was burnt down; it was rebuilt in 978 AD. The actual grandiose Basilica was not begun until 1063 under the Dogate of the Contarini. St. Mark's then became the religious symbol of Venice and of a Christianity receptive to Eastern influence. The fourth crusade set out from the Basilica; here Barbarossa and Pope Alexander III were reconciled; here the sailors drawn up in battle-order were blessed before sailing to fight against Genoa. For 900 years the Basilica has kept its original shape: a Greek cross with five domes designed by an unknown artist, possibly a Greek. But for centuries, at least until the 16th century, it was constantly enriched and added to in many styles.

The façade

The unusual façade has two series of arches: five on top and five below, the latter jutting out. Below these are five great portals with bas reliefs depicting sacred scenes and artists and crafts-men at work. The five upper arches are crowned by decorative Gothic statues and pinnacles. The central arch has been glassed in to let light into the Basilica. The famous four bronze horses stand on the tribune. Of uncertain, if much debated origin – Greek perhaps – Roman of the 4th or 3rd centuries or even of the age of Constantine or even by Lysippus, the quadriga (a chariot drawn by four horses abreast) came to Venice as part of the booty from the crusade of 1204. Half a century later it was raised on the Basilica as a symbol of Venetian liberty. In 1797 Napoleon, sacking the city, had the horses transferred to France and placed in the Tuileries. They were taken back to Venice in 1815. On the façade there is now a replica, the original having been placed inside the church.

The four bronze horses

Looking up, you see the five onion-shaped domes. At their summits are placed Byzantine-style lanterns with decorative crosses. Centuries ago each dome was covered by another taller lead-plated wooden one. This touch helps to accentuate the decidedly Byzantine aspect of the church.

Mosaic on the façade representing Christ in glory and the Final Judgement

The interior of the Basilica

On entering the Basilica you are dazzled by the wealth of sumptuous arches, domes, mosaics and precious decorations. First of all you notice the impressive mosaic pavement, like an enormous Oriental carpet covering the whole church.

The Pala D'Oro

The multicoloured tesserae form images of beasts and strange birds; the most compelling scenes of this 'narrative' are in the transepts, particularly in the righthand one. The richness of the mosaics is the result of two different techniques: one using regular tesserae, the other placing the tesserae at different angles. In the heart of the Basilica is the iconostasis (the screen separating the faithful from the chancel) where is placed the high altar. The iconostasis is 13th century Gothic, lavishly decorated by statues of the Apostles and Saints by the brothers Dalle Masegne and by a monumental silver crucifix.

Here is the heart of the temple because of the urn placed beneath the altar containing the relics of St. Mark. In the past they were kept in the crypt. Behind the altar stands the famous Golden Altarpiece, an indisputable masterpiece of the goldsmith's art; it is made up of three thousand precious stones and eighty Byzantine enamels. The whole is mounted in a Gothic setting signed by Gian Paolo Boninsegna.

The Iconostasis: gotic structure of the 13th century

Made up of panels and enamels commissioned in Costantinople, the Golden Altarpiece was further enriched between the 10th and 13th centuries, until in 1345, under Doge Dandolo it achieved its present form. This gem is part of the so-called Treasury of St. Mark's, made up of splendid objects such as invaluable icons and sacred vestments. They clearly show the unmistakable influence of Byzantium on Venetian art and culture and are now kept in a tower of the old Doges' Palace. The baldachin above the high altar is supported by four alabaster columns sculpted with New Testament scenes.

The mosaics

The magic power of the Basilica resides above all in the admirable, endless mosaics; the whole temple seems to be lined in glittering gold. The work is collective and therefore anonymous: ingenious craftsmen and masters of mosaic – inspired by the mosaics in Ravenna and Byzantium – created it long before famous artists of the 15th and 16th centuries contributed their designs.

Detail of the pavement

The most beautiful mosaics in the basilica are those in the arch towards the nave, called the arch of the Passion, showing episodes from the life of Christ. Another equally outstanding mosaic is in the atrium, in the dome dedicated to Genesis, where the Creation of the World is depicted in concentric circles. The visitor cannot ignore that the most revered image in the Basilica is the Vergine Nicopeia (Virgin of Victory). It was certainly taken from Constantinople and was for centuries the symbol of Venice victorious over the seas. It is an old Byzantine painting perhaps of the 10th century.
Precious stones surround it in a gold frame divided into sixteen panels.

13

The Doges' palace

A splendid building, rose-tinted and rich in lacy arcading, this palace is the biggest civic construction in Venice. For centuries it was the home of the Doge and seat of the Republic's political power. Here gathered the political, administrative and judicial assemblies. It also harboured the armouries and the prisons. The eyes of Europe contemplated this splendid symbol and seat of an almost perfect government, uniting as it did a monarchy (a Doge for life), an aristocracy (nobles in the senate) and a democracy (the Great Council first consisting of a thousand members and later of two thousand). It was well amalgamated, as no one power dominated over the other. Within the palace great artists and sculptors illustrated the power and glory of the Venetian Republic on large canvasses, on arches, staircases and monuments.

venice

The building

The outside of the Doges' Palace is impressive. It was built between the 14th and 16th centuries over a pre-existing turreted castle. Many hands took part in its construction: Dalle Masegne, Pietro Lamberti, Antonio Rizzo and P. Lombardo. With great ingenuity its façade overthrows all architectural rules by placing delicate lacy arcading which supports a mass of masonry above. The palace is divided into three orders: first a portico with pointed arches, on top a loggia decorated with quatrefoil roundels, surmounted by a wall with beautiful decorations in dark pink. White marble crennelations in the Byzantine-Venetian style crown the façade.

A visit to the rooms

The courtyard

The first courtyard is airy, sumptuous and solemn, and is approached through the Porta della Carta, in flowery Gothic style, by Bon (1438). The gateway is crowned by a winged lion and by the statue of the Doge Francesco Foscari. The interior façades are in Gothic-Renaissance style; to the north the porch and the Foscari Arch stand out, in front the Staircase of the Giants with the statues by Sansovino of Neptune and Mars; above is the façade of the Clock. The Staircase of the Censors leads to the Piano delle Logge opening onto the courtyard, dominated by the Loggia Foscari towards the Piazzetta. The Golden Staircase, work of Sansovino and Scarpagnino, leads to the upper floors where are the main rooms and the Doge's luxurious apartments, the vault of which is decorated with marble and gilded stuccoes by Alessandro Vittoria. Inside the palace many activities took place, so that by visiting it you will get a good idea of how the Republic functioned: the apartments of the Doge (therefore a court as well), offices and chancelleries, reception rooms, armouries, tribunals, prisons. The most important rooms are on the upper floors. Here where the Doges once lived are Carpaccio's painting of St. Mark's Lion, works of Bellini and the strange paintings of the Flemish Hieronymus Bosch like The Ascent to Heaven.

The largest and most opulent room in the palace is that of the Maggior Consiglio (The Great Council) where more than a thousand Venetian nobles gathered to elect the Doge. At the back of the room, over the elegant tribune is Tintoretto's huge Paradise (7x22 metres). Reflecting the glory of Venice are Paolo Veronese's Apotheosis of Venice, works by Palma the Younger and by Bassano. In the Room of the Scrutinio where the votes were counted, are The Last Judgement by Palma the Younger and the continuation of the series of portraits of the Doges (which start in the Room of the Maggior Consiglio). On the next floor is the Room of the Four Doors where there is Titian's Doge Grimali adoring faith and a fresco by Tintoretto which evokes the founding of Venice. After this we find the Room of the Collegio, reception place for ambassadors. The Room of the Senate is long and narrow, and the walls are lined with decorative wooden panels; the fine ceiling and the walls are decorated with works by Tintoretto and Palma the Younger in rich gold frames. In the austere Room of the Consiglio dei Dieci (Council of Ten), where gathered the fearful court which tried political crimes, are excellent paintings, some by Veronese. The Room of the Bussola (Compass) is extremely interesting because of the typical double door where you can still see the boxes (called the Mouths of the Lions) where anonymous letters were placed denouncing criminals. Beyond the Room of the Three Heads of the Consiglio dei Dieci (elected from amongst the Ten for the period of a month) and the Room of the Inquisitori di Stato (Government Inquisitors) you can visit the Armoury which holds a collection of arms (booty of war and those meant for the defence of the Republic). The Armoury displays swords,

The Golden staircase

halberds, culverins, lances, the armour of Henry IV of France, two armours of the Sforza, a "quick-firing" gun with twenty barrels and the bronze bust of Francesco Morosini. Under the Room of the Avongaria are the eighteen dungeons of the Pozzi where for over two centuries prisoners were tormented by suffering. Beneath the leaden roof are the prison cells, called the Piombi, notorious for being narrow and excruciatingly hot. The visit to this sumptuous palace concludes with the Bridge of Sighs, symbol of the torments of all those who dared oppose the government.

❮❮ The bridge of sighs
from prison to romantic spot

Venice is famous for its many bridges, but one in particular attracts tourists, as once it brought fear to the hearts of ruffians.
The Bridge of Sighs connected the court rooms in the Doges' Palace to the nearby new prisons

– completed at the beginning of the 17th century – over the canal. It had already been ordered in the 16th century when the infamous prisons of the palace were judged to be too narrow and unhealthy. And so Antonio Da Ponte and then Antonio Contin built the bridge, later to be called The Bridge of Sighs. It is built of Istrian stone with internal corridors lengthwise divided by a wall. The condemned had to cross the bridge.

The fearful prisons of the Doges' Palace were still in use: both the eighteen dungeons of the Pozzi (the wells) on the ground floor, and the Piombi (lead cells) under the roof.

The latter got its name from the fact that the ceiling was plated in lead. In both these prisons, damp, extremely narrow and unhealthy, the prisoners lived out a hell on earth.

Usually they were brought here after being tortured in the "Room of Torments", as we learn from the well-known memoirs of Giacomo Casanova, libertine and traveller, condemned for licentious conduct and insults to religion.

Casanova made a spectacular escape in 1756. Even today, amidst all the splendours of the palace we can still see the lions' mouths in which were slipped the odious anonymous letters of informers. On the prison walls you can still read the prisoners' dramatic messages. ❯❯

The important basilicas

Basilica della Salute

Near St. Mark's, in the heart of Venice, the Basilica della Salute stands on the edge of the Grand Canal. Like many churches in Venice, the Basilica della Salute was built in thanks-giving for the deliverance from a plague, in this case the terrible pestilence of 1630 a year later, the Venetians decided to build a church which was to be, and is, and apotheosis of the Virgin. The construction was entrusted to the young architect Baldassarre Longhena, who later embellished Venice with many buildings, such as the Ca'Rezzonico and the Ca'Pesaro on the Grand Canal. The style of this church challenged Roman baroque, that of Borromini and of Bernini. The Venetian baroque had a new look, original touches and showed the influence of Palladio.

The Basilica rises over the lagoon, reflecting its bright surface in the water.

The grandiose, imposing baroque exterior contrasts with the simple, dignified interior, a vast circular space surrounded by six chapels.

There are eight façades, two domes (the one over the apse is smaller) and two slender bell towers; a triumphal arch in the central façade marks the entrance and is approached by a monumental marble flight of steps.

The eloquent swirling Baroque takes solid form in the hundred – and more – statues that crown the cusps, in the huge volutes that function as buttresses for the dome (the Venetians named them "Big Ears") in the white Istrian marble that decorates this complex and magnificent building; all of which makes this church the very symbol of solemn yet magnificent piety.

Basilica della Salute

Basilica della Salute, general view

We now enter the church. The high dome (over 60 metres high) with its drum pierced by large windows sheds a beautiful light on the circular aisle, decorated with an astonishing polychrome marble floor using an intricate spiral design framing thirty two roses, symbolising the Virgin's rosary.

The whole Basilica pays homage to the Virgin; the statue that stands on the tympanum outside, The Madonna and Child, is dedicated to her as is the Madonna della Salute, over the high altar.

The latter is a Byzantine painting brought to Venice in 1672 by Francesco Morosini from the distant island of Candia.

After many years, in 1687 the church was finally completed by the architect Antonio Gaspari. Great works of art are kept in the chapels and sacristies. Titian is represented by his St. Mark enthroned between Saints, and by the three canvases on the ceiling depicting Cain and Abel, Sacrifice of Isaac, David and Goliath. Tintoretto is represented by the famous Wedding in Cana, a 16th century rendition of Christ's miracle painted in 1561 for the refectory of the Padri Crociferi.

Other churches

Other churches close to the Basilica della Salute are well worth a visit. On the Guidecca there is the Church of the Redentore, begun by Palladio in 1577 and finished in 1592.

It has a single nave and a series of beautiful chapels with paintings by Bassano, Tintoretto, Palma the Younger, Veronese and his workshop.

In the sacristy is the "Baptism of Christ" by Veronese. It is delightful to be in Venice on the third Sunday in July when the Feast of the Redeemer is celebrated and the whole city gathers here. Many treasures are kept in the Church of Santa Maria del Rosario, also called of the Jesuates. The church witnessed the suppression of the order of the Jesuates because of the latter's scandalous behaviour.

It went to the Dominicans and became the main temple of that fighting order.

Inside there are many works of Gian Battista Tiepolo, a master of the Venetian 18th century.

When glancing at the lagoon you inevitably see the golden ball of the Punta della Dogana (called "da mar", "from sea", as opposed to the other Venetian customs house called "de tera", "from land").

The Fondamenta delle Zattere (so called because here timber was unloaded from large rafts) offers the opportunity for a charming stroll.

Basilica dei Frari

The Basilica dei Frari is a large complex in brick and marble; in fact it is the biggest one in Venice after St. Mark's. It is a sort of pantheon containing as it does so many splendid noble tombs and a large art collection. It is made up of the church, skirted by two vast cloisters, a bell tower (one of the highest in Venice) and of the ex-convent, which contains the State Archives, among the most famous in the world. If the church of the Jesuates is the apotheosis of the Dominican order, the Frari (Venetian dialect for "i frati", "the friars") is the domain of the Franciscan order and its history.

The Franciscans came to Venice in the early 13th century and were given a plot of land where they built a modest church, enriched in the mid-14th century. At the beginning of the 15th century the actual Basilica replaced the earlier one; it is imposing, majestic, in brick but enriched with white marble decorations.

There are many masterpieces inside this vast church. Over the main altar hangs Titian's magnificent Assumption; in the Pesaro chapel another equally famous work by Titian, the innovative Pesaro Altarpiece; Donatello's only documented work in Venice, the wooden statue of St. John the Baptist (there is another St. John the Baptist by Sansovino in another part of the Basilica); in the apse of the Sacristy Giovanni Bellini's triptych of the Madonna and Child between Saints Nicholas, Peter, Mark and Benedict, perhaps the painter's greatest work; last but not least the Virgin by the 14th century Venetian painter Paolo Veneziano.

There is yet another unusual masterpiece: the grandiose wooden choir. It contains 124 stalls and a series of statues and carvings by the famous Cozzi family of Vicenza. The choir is unique as so few works of this kind have come down to us in such good condition.

The soaring plain interior of the church is enriched by the seven south choir chapels, and the two later Renaissance side chapels, commissioned by the Corner and Emiliani families.

Here, as in the nave, there are numerous mausoleums (it shares this characteristic with the Church of Santa Croce in Florence), making a pantheon of illustrious Venetians. If not the most beautiful, the most famous are those (placed in front of each other) dedicated to Titian and to the neo-classical sculptor Antonio Canova.

The latter, a high pyramid decorated by weeping figures – they guard the heart of the artist in a porphyry urn – had been designed by Canova himself as a mausoleum to Titian (he died of the plague in Venice in 1576), but it was never built. The disciples of Canova, however, eventually built it for their master. The disciples of Titian, who had asked to be buried in the Frari, built him a mausoleum. Another illustrious Venetian who rests here is Claudio Monteverdi who for thirty years was the choir master at St. Mark's and is the composer of so much religious music.

The Basilica dei Frari, interior

The Basilica dei Frari, Titian, Assumption

To the left and right of the presbytery there are many tombs. One to Doge Francesco Foscari by Antonio and Paolo Bregno, a mixture of Gothic and Renaissance styles.

One to the Doge Nicolò Tron by Antonio Rizzo, considered a Renaissance masterpiece and perhaps the most grandiose sarcophagus in the city. Bregno also sculptured a monument to the Condottiero Melchiorre Trevisan (in the Trevisan Chapel) and one of Frederico Corner (in the Corner Chapel) in the style of Donatello, the latter is an excellent example of Venetian Renaissance work.

But maybe the most magnificent mausoleum in the Frari is one to the Doge Giovanni Pesaro in the north aisle. It is an ornate yet elegant Baroque work in multicoloured marble, conceived by the greatly represented Venetian architect Baldassarre Longhena. Leaving the Frari, the pulse of so many events in Venice, we will go to another large church and so conclude our visit of the churches.

The Basilica of Santi Giovanni e Paolo is an excellent example of religious Gothic architecture and stands in the square by the same name in the Castello district. It is placed between the equestrian statue of Colleoni (whose request was denied to have it placed in St. Mark's Square) and the 15th century façade of the Scuola Grande di San Marco.

The statue is a work by Andrea Verrocchio, cast in bronze by Alessandro Leopardi (1496) who also added the ornate pedestal.

Do not overlook other equally interesting churches such as Santa Maria dei Derelitti. The façade of this church is by Longhena and the overhanging grotesque stone masks are by Le Court. Inside is the Sacrifice of Isaac by Giambattista Tiepolo. There is also the Church of the Mendicanti and the Church of San Francesco della Vigna.

Basilica of Santi Giovanni e Paolo

The Basilica of Santi Giovanni e Paolo is a reminder of power and misery. The equestrian statue of the Condottiero Bartolomeo Colleoni, head of the Venetian army in the 15th century, dominates the small square. Very near is the Canale dei Mendicanti (Beggars) which takes its name from the nearby almshouse.

The magnificent Basilica took two hundred years to build.

Begun by the Dominicans around 1360 it was consecrated in 1430; the construction of the new façade was interrupted towards the end of the century thus leaving the doorway unfinished.

This church – one of great significance – was for a long time the favoured burial place of the Doges.

Beneath sumptuous monuments lie the Doges Alvise and Pietro Mocenigo (the first tomb is considered to be one of the most interesting Renaissance works of Pietro Lombardo), Pasquale Malipiero and Andrea Vendramin, whose monuments are also by Lombardo.

The organ is still in use and is the work of Gaetano Gallido, the celebrated Venetian organ maker who lived between the 18th and 19th centuries. Here are also the tombs of the celebrated Venetian artists Bellini and Lorenzo Lotto. The skin of Marc' Antonio Bragadin, a valiant Venetian who fell in battle in Cyprus and was skinned by the Turks, is kept here in an urn.

After paying homage to the tombs of illustrious Venetians, after admiring the coloured light

21

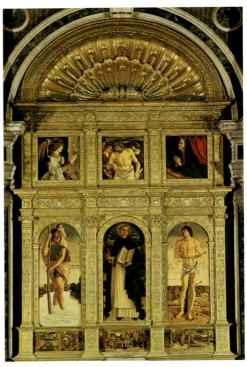

The Basilica of Santi Giovanni e Paolo; at left: Monument to the Senator G. Bonzio; at right: Bellini, polyptych of St. Vincent Ferrer

reflected from the church façade, after listening – if you are lucky enough – to music played on the large organ, you can now admire the master-pieces kept in the beautiful church.

Over the second altar hangs the polyptych of St. Vincent Ferrer by the young Bellini, one of the great paintings of the Early Renaissance in which can be discerned influences of Mantegna, brother-in-law of the artist. The three panels represent the great Dominican mission preacher flanked by St. Christopher carrying the baby Christ and by St. Sebastian.

Noteworthy are the smaller panels above the central painting depicting an Angel of the Annunciation and the magnificent Dead Christ between Two Angels.

The "predelle" illustrate episodes from the life of St. Vincent. Not to be missed are three works by Veronese fitted in the ceiling of the Chapel of the Rosary, restored at the beginning of this century after a devastating fire.

To conclude this rapid sketch of Venetian churches, it must be said there are many more well worth a visit. They are all distinguished either by a feeling of religious fervour within or by works of art.

So if you still have the time, visit the Church of the Angelo Raffaele in Dorsoduro, the unusual Renaissance style Santa Maria dei Miracoli and the neo-classical Church of the Maddalena with its characteristic green dome.

Finally there is the tiny church of San Giocomo di Rialto near the famous bridge by the same name. This church is at once the smallest and the oldest in Venice.

The bell tower and portico are in wood. On the outside wall of the apse is an amusing inscription urging the merchants – this was their district – to use fair prices and give correct weights.

Church of Santa Maria dei Miracoli

Museums

The Accademy Galleries

The Accademy Galleries contain the history and glory of five centuries of Venetian painting. As you ascend the 18th century grand staircase prepare yourself for the illustrated stories from St. Ursula's life by Carpaccio, the touching Christ by Bellini, the unsolved mysteries of the Tempest by Giorgione, the rich architecture and lavish velvets of the Supper in the House of Levi by Veronese. The collective works in the Galleries, from the 14th century Lorenzo and Paolo Veneziano to the 18th century "vedutisti" (painters of panoramic views) Guardi and Canaletto, illustrate with the typically Venetian use of colour – as opposed to the Tuscan use of line – the city, its faith, its pomp, its happy and diversified society. The Accademy was founded in 1750 as the "Academy of Painters and Sculptors" and was managed first by Piazzetta and later by Tiepolo. In the time of Napoleon (1817) the picture gallery was opened to the public. At the end of World War II the museum was reconstructed by the architect Carlo Scarpa. The masterpieces hanging here are the triumphant story of "colour", an important chapter in the 700 years of Italian painting. Paolo Veneziano's Coronation of the Virgin and a large polyptych also by Veneziano inaugurate the history of art in Venice and its transition (at the end of the 14th century) from the solemn Byzantine style to the new flamboyant Gothic. Between the 14th and 15th centuries Lorenzo (a disciple but not a relation of Paolo) Veneziano's Annunciation and four Saints stands out by its sinuous movements and typically Gothic love of gold. In the 15th century the Bellini family dominate Venetian painting; while Gentile is an able portrait and landscape painter (as his remarkable Miracle of the fallen Cross bears witness), the great works of Giovanni express a deep melancholy as shown in the wonderful Pietà of Christ and his mother against a gentle Vicentine background (in which her face is old and unlovely), the enormous Altarpiece of St. Job

Carpaccio, Legend
of St. Ursula, detail

venice

Giorgione,
The Tempest

[1487] (in which through cleverly playing with perspective the Virgin appears enthroned and inaccessible among the solemn figures of saints) and the down-to-earth Madonna of the Alberetti, so called because of two "alberetti" (small trees) framing the whole. Do not forget, amongst so many masterpieces, to admire the St. George, a work of rare perfection, by Mantegna.

And now we come to Vittore Carpaccio, the great pictorial narrator of 15th century Venice. Nine canvasses, painted at the end of the century, form the most important cycle by this artist and relate the Legend of St. Ursula, wife of an English prince, who goes accompanied by eleven thousand virgins on a pilgrimage to various sanctuaries. Carpaccio shows in a Venetian setting, even though the events take place elsewhere, the magnificence of the processions, Kings, ambassadors, Popes and snatches from weddings, so relating the life of the Venetian nobles; air and light crowd his canvasses. They are in sharp contrast to the work of the silent mysterious Giorgione – the greatest Venetian artist of them all. The Accademy has his greatest masterpiece The Tempest, once known as The Gypsy and the Soldier. For a long time it proved difficult to interpret its symbolic and narrative meaning. Because of the white child in the painting there were suggestions that it might allude to the myth of Paris or of Moses or it might even be an allegory of Venus genitrix. What is important is the mystery that surrounds the figures.

They form part of a stormy, yet serene, landscape which tends to dominate the painting.

Giorgione's use of colour (achieved by his use of special varnishes) lends an unprecedented luminosity as the other masterpiece The Old Woman demonstrates. The latter is an allegory of the ages of man, as declares the scroll in the woman's hands. It is painted realistically but not without a deep symbolic significance.

Three great Venetian painters represent the 16th century: Paolo Veronese, Tintoretto and Titian. Titian's vigorous colours exalt the massive images that, from his early to his later paintings, go from a serene richness to an agonised movement. The Venetians loved Titian so much – he was official painter to the Serenissima – that when in old age he died of the plague he was spared a communal grave and buried at the Frari instead. Here in this museum hangs his last Pietà (1576). In this painting all traces of drawing have disappeared; only dark colours dominate (the bloody figure of Christ is rendered with thick dabs of white paint) and so create an atmosphere of anxious questioning. There is another Titian hanging here: St. John the Baptist. After witnessing Titian's despair, we are pleasantly soothed by Paolo Veronese's cheerful feast in the large Supper in the house of Levi. Veronese was the official court painter after Titian's death. The title was originally "The Last Supper", but the Inquisition ordered it to be changed as he supposedly placed profane figures next to Christ. The painting has a festive setting: in front of three arches there is a throng of people in various attitudes creating an atmosphere of festivity and ritual which almost anticipates melodrama.

Tintoretto is represented by the exquisite canvasses from the cycle of St. Mark. Outstanding are St. Mark's Miracle, where the saint sweeps down to liberate one of his followers from martyrdom, and the beautiful and scenographic Transport of the body of St. Mark. Noteworthy are the inspired portraits of Doges and Procurators.

Pause at the works of the minor painters of the 17th century (Strozzi, Maffei and Mazzone) which lead to the harmonious views of the great Venetian vedutisti and in particular to the works of Longhi, Guardi, Canaletto, Tiepolo, Rosalba Carriera (an expert in the use of pastels). The genre painters Pietro Longhi and his son Alessandro illustrate Venetian society accurately and in a lively manner. The figures illustrate the striking originality of the various personages. Admire the rare beauty of the Fortune Teller.

The artist Rosalba Carriera throws light on the Venetian world in her pastel drawings. Canaletto who paints with photographic accuracy is the best illustrator of 18th century Venice. Francesco Guardi paints the ephemereal with melancholy and accuracy.

Canaletto, view of the lagoon at St. Mark's

School of St. George

Carpaccio,
St. Augustine
in his study

Nine large paintings by Carpaccio, now displayed on the ground floor, transform the antique Scuola degli Schiavoni into a spectacular pictorial narrative. The Dalmatians (called "Schiavoni", "slaves", because their territory was the first to be conquered by the Venetian Republic when they arrived in Venice), formed a "scuola" (a guild of various workers and ethnic groups) in 1451 and chose, as its seat, this building. Carpaccio was asked to decorate it with nine canvasses dedicated to the three patron saints of Dalmatia: Saints George, Tryphon and Jerome, the translator of the Bible. The outstanding cycle of Carpaccio's works should be seen. The highlights are the two splendid canvasses representing St. George and the Dragon and the Triumph of St. George. In the first painting of the cycle of St. George, Carpaccio represents the fair knight on a dark horse in the act of piercing, with his long lance, the dragon. The lance divides and balances the painting. In the following painting the dragon is dragged into the square and killed. The canvasses of the trilogy of St. Jerome are extraordinary because of the richness of the scenery where scenes from Venetian

life are placed in Eastern landscapes with their palms and lions (everything in Venice has a flavour of the East); especially the Death of St. Jerome with its naked saints standing on the bare earth surrounded by friars in deep blue cloaks. Worthy of admiration is the canvas of St. Augustine in his Study (listening to the voice of St. Jerome). In Carpaccio's works, a jubilant narrative links a love for scenery, to the frequent use of Eastern elements (perhaps due to his journey into that part of the world).

Scuola di San Rocco

In 1564 there was a competition for the embellishment of the Scuola Grande di San Rocco, which was built by Antonio Scarpagnino, after a drawing by Bartolomeo Bon, a few decades earlier, next to the Church of San Rocco.

Many great artists participated in the competition, among whom Veronese, Salviati, Zuccari and Tintoretto, who won the competition.

The Scuola has numerous canvasses by Tintoretto, probably the best examples of his work. The contrast between light and shadow and the dramatic use of foreshortening result in scenes rich in pathos and force.

Tintoretto, Crucifixion

More than thirty large canvasses are displayed on the ground floor and on the first floor in the Sala dell'Albergo and the Salone Maggiore (twentyone on the ceiling and twelve on the walls).

The story of St. Roch runs parallel to the life of Christ, from the Annunciation (notice the superb archangel descending from the heavens surrounded by white angels) to the terrible Massacre of the Innocents, rich in colour and dense with figures, Christ in front of Pilate, Ecce homo, Way to Calvary culminating in the enormous Crucifixion (5x12 metres), the most extraordinary painting in the Scuola di San Rocco.

The thrill and tense drama of the events depicted by Tintoretto must not prevent the visitor from admiring two other works here placed: an Annunciation (1525) by Titian and Abraham and the Angels by the young Gian Battista Tiepolo.

The Church and School of San Rocco were built and dedicated to this saint who was thought to be, especially in Venice, a protector against the plague.

Ca' Rezzonico: Museum of the Venetian Settecento

On to the charming Museum of the Settecento, which is on the Grand Canal in the vast Ca' Rezzonico palace. It was built in two stages by two architects between 1667 and 1751

The façade

for the procurator Bartolomeo Bon to a design by the great architect Baldassarre Longhena. But he died before it had risen above the first floor, and the Bon family fell into financial difficulties. Another patron appeared in the person of Gian Battista Rezzonico, whose son Carlo became pope Clement XIII. Massari was commissioned to complete the building and once completed it was used for feasts and official receptions.

It is easy to imagine the beautiful courtyard and the grand staircase as it once was: thronged with happy, chatty, elegant high society Venetians. There are many works of art to see, but the 18th century produced many artistic achievements other than paintings: the ornate and sumptuous rooms (the huge ballroom is two storeys high), the remarkable furniture carved by the famous Andrea Brustolon, the

Carpaccio, Two venetian ladies

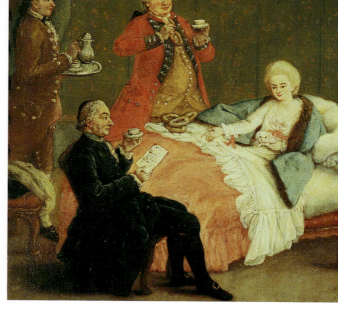

Pietro Longhi, Morning cup of chocolate

tapestries, the numerous glass objects by the great Venetian glass-makers (in particular the outstanding chandelier with twenty branches by Guiseppe Briati), a puppet theatre and a pharmacy on the third floor. Two geniuses preside over the picture gallery and the frescoes of Ca' Rezzonico: Giovan Battista Tiepolo and Pietro Longhi. In thirty paintings the latter illustrates satirically and in detail the everyday activities of the Venetians: Morning cup of chocolate, Lady's toilette, La polenta (gruel), The painter's studio – they are as telling now as they were two hundred years ago. There are also two paintings by Guardi: The Lounge and Nuns' Parlour, both perfect illustrations of faith and worldliness ambiguously mixed together. The Tiepolo, father and son, are famous for different reasons. The father, Giovan Battista, whose luminous frescoes are on the ceiling of the Throne Room, for his Allegory of Merit. The son Gian Domenico's best paintings are in this museum: the charming, cheerful rendering of fashionable Venetian society Portego del Mondo Nuovo and Minuet in the villa. And even more expressive are the illustrations of the clowns: The home of the acrobats, The rest of the clowns and The clown in love.

The Correr Museum

Carpaccio, Portrait of man with a red beret

Our visit to the museums in the city takes us back to the city centre in St. Mark's Square where is the Correr Museum in the rooms of the Procuratie Nuove. It is worth a visit if only to admire the Man with a red beret, a great and mysterious portrait by Carpaccio. If he was a great narrator in the St. Ursula cycle, here he reveals himself as a disturbing psychologist. There is also a Pietà by Cosmè Tura, in which Christ is portrayed as half-child half-adult (in a strong expressionistic style) lying in the arms of his mother (influenced by Flemish realism). The two paintings are on the last floor of the museum. There are also masterpieces by Bellini, Two Venetian Ladies (formerly known as the Two Courtesans) by Vittore Carpaccio, Madonna and Child by Lorenzo Lotto, and works by Lorenzo Veneziano.

27

The Grand Canal

The Grand Canal is, of course, the centre of attraction. It divides the city into two parts forming a large upside down "s". It begins in the Piazzale Roma and from the Station flows into the luminous Bacino di San Marco. It is four kilometres long, but 1.8 kilometres as the crow flies. It has been sung by poets and writers and millions of tourists go up and down it nowadays. And here it was, in the golden age, that the wealthy society of the Serenissima built their palaces, all competing in luxury and elegance. Palaces yes, but also churches and gardens, their elongated shapes and colours reflected in the waters of the canal. It is an astonishing and unique place, urban and maritime, where everything takes place with the calmness of the sea.

The left bank

The Dogana da Mar (customs house), work of Giuseppe Benoni constructed in the mid-17th century, stands at the far end of the promontory next to a little turret surmounted by a golden sphere (symbol of good fortune). Beyond it is the Chiesa della Salute and the 15th century Palazzo Dario, richly ornamented with multicoloured marbles by Pietro Lombardo. Further along is the Palazzo Venier dei Leone (mid-18th century), now the Guggenheim Art Gallery, followed by the Palazzo Contarini dal Zaffo, a Late Renaissance building with high narrow lodges and decorative multicoloured marbles. And so to the Accademy Galleries which is in the palace restructured at the beginning of the 19th century. After the Palazzo Contarini degli Scrigni there is the Palazzo Loredan, called the Palace of the Ambassador because in the 17th century it was the residence of the Austrian ambassador to Venice, a glorious example of 15th century Gothic with mullioned windows and quatrefoils. The following palaces should also be visited: the Palazzo Ca' Rezzonico by Longhena, presently the seat of the Museum of the Settecento, the Palazzo Giustinian and the Palazzo Foscari (today housing the University Ca' Foscari), two similar and spectacular buildings divided by a narrow street. The Palazzo Foscari is one of the most imposing palaces of the Grand Canal with its lofty upper floors and a central room with big mullioned windows. Then there is the Palazzo Balbi where Napoleon stayed, now the seat of the Consiglio Regionale Veneto (Regional Council), with its two typical obelisks on the roof. It was built at the end of the 16th century, probably following a design of Alessandro Vittoria, and is already suggestive of the Baroque style. Still on the left bank is the Palazzo Pisani-Moretta in the Gothic style: enriched by big mullioned windows and typical little terraces (the interior of the palace has not been modified and is still lived in by the Pisani family).

Then there is the Palazzo Barbarigo della Terrazza, so-called because of its splendid garden terrace. The Renaissance style Palazzo Grimani with its arches and loggias of the Lombardo school (16th century). After the Palazzo dei Camerlenghi we come to the Palazzo Corner della Regina which stands alone between two canals and was constructed in 1724 by Domenico Rossi on a pre-existing building where Catherine Corner, queen of Cyprus, was born in 1454. The Palazzo Pesaro, one of the most imposing on the Grand Canal, is now the seat of the Museum of Modern Art (containing works of Matisse, Chagall, Klimt) and the Museum of Oriental Art. The palace was begun by Longhena at the end of the 17th century and finished at the beginning of the following century by Antonio Gaspari, whose work is a superb example of Baroque architecture. The Church of San Stae which is dedicated to St. Eustace was probably founded before 1000 AD and constructed in the early 18th century. Beyond it is the Palazzo Belloni-Battaglia. This is a work of the 17th century by Baldassarre Longhena who restructured the interior and the façade of an already existing Gothic edifice adding new motifs such as coat-of-arms, gables and two round apertures. Finally before the Church of San Simeon Piccolo, with its typical green dome in imitation of the Pantheon in Rome, is the Depositi or Fondaco del Megio which was used for centuries as a granary. This is the end of the journey along the left bank of the Grand Canal. You can repeat the journey again, this time to admire the palaces and churches on the right bank.

Ca' Pesaro

« The gondola
most famous boat in the world

The gondola and the gondolier are typically and uniquely Venetian.
The asymmetrical gondola (with one side curving out much more than the other) is normally eleven metres long and a little less than a metres and a half wide. It is made of two hundred and eighty pieces of wood, usually oak except for the rowlock in walnut and the oar in beech wood. It must have a curve in proportion to the gondolier's weight.
There are about four hundred gondoliers today; the occupation is handed down from father

to son. In the past they wore rich clothes, but now a black suit, a straw hat and a striped shirt is the norm.
Today the art of building gondolas is in the hands of a few remaining expert carpenters working in small workshops called "squeri". Once built, the boat is given at least seven coats of black varnish whose formula, they say, is secret.
The gondola has an iron decoration on the prow called "ferro", which only took its present shape two hundred years ago.
The ferro has six toothed projections representing the six "sestieri" (districts) of the city.
A delicate part of the boat is the curved "forcola" (rowlock), used as a rest for the oar. According to Venetian custom, the rowing gondolier stands at the stern with one leg forward and looking towards the prow.
The gondolas used to be brightly painted, adorned with draperies and statues – befitting the ostentation of Venetian society.
Through a series of edicts in the 16th century, the Signoria eliminated the ostentation: it was only allowed to be painted in black. »

Ca' d'Oro, façade

The right bank

Palazzo Grassi,
façade

Palazzo Grassi,
façade

Among the first palaces here are: the Contarini Fasan, a little gem of flowery Gothic art from the end of the 15th century, and the Palazzo Gritti, now a hotel of international fame which at one time was actually decorated with frescoes by Giorgione. Then the Palazzo Corner della Ca' Grande, Palazzo Giustinian Lolin, a work of the 17th century by Longhena built over a pre-existing Gothic palace (this explains the elongated shape of its windows). Then the world famous Palazzo Grassi, commissioned by the wealthy family of the same name, which was built in mid-18th century by Giorgio Massari. One of its façades looks over the Campo San Samuele and it is today the seat of prestigious exhibitions thanks to the Agnelli family. Palazzo Contarini delle Figure (early 16th century), taking its name from the two caryatids that uphold the balcony, is attributed to Scarpagnino. Then there are the two famous Old and New Mocenigo Palaces commissioned by the great Venetian family of the same name. Two identical and specular palaces were later joined to them. Giordano Bruno lived there in 1592. Here he was denounced, so the story goes, to the Holy Inquisition. After the Gothic Palazzo Garzoni and the Palazzo Corner Spinelli is the Palazzo Benzon, famous as

Ca' d'Oro, façade

a meeting place for social and literary purposes between the 18th and 19th centuries. Here Foscolo, Canova and Lord Byron used to meet. The Fondaco dei Tedeschi is an interesting building with an internal courtyard and open galleries. At one time it actually had frescoes on its main façade by Giorgione, but they have completely disappeared; the facade was modified in the 19th century. It takes its name from the fact that it was used at one time by the German community, once very active in Venice. There follows the Ca' da Mosto, example of an old 12th century building. It was first built as a one-storey house and warehouse in the Byzantine fashion, and then more floors were added in the 17th century. Initially it was used for commercial purposes as depots and dwelling; later it became the famous Venetian inn, "Del Leon Bianco" (The White Lion) that offered accommodation to illustrious clients from the 16th to the 18th centuries. Another building famous throughout the world, Ca' d'Oro, was built in mid-15th century by Marino Contarini with ostentatious use of gold and a multicoloured façade, hence its name. It is one of the purest examples of Venetian flowery Gothic due to its two rows of open galleries. The Palazzo Gussoni Grimani is one of the most striking palaces along this side of the Grand Canal, and is well worth a careful look (it once had frescoes by Tintoretto on the façade). Ca' Vendramin Calergi is a splendid example of Venetian Renaissance architecture. Palazzo Labia, today housing the Rai (Italian Broadcasting Corporation), is an 18th century work by the architect Tremignon. It has delightful frescoes inside by G. Battista Tiepolo. Beyond is the Church of San Geremia, an extremely old building that was restructured in the second half of the 18th century. Our walk concludes with the Palazzo Flangini, a 17th century building by Giuseppe Sardi.

venice

❮❮ The Carnival

the great festival of Venice

Venice means carnival. It is unrivalled for its invention of disguises, costumes, dances, masques, and for its atmosphere of fun.

The carnival used to start on the day after Christmas and ended on Shrove Tuesday when the bells of San Francesco della Vigna proclaimed the beginning of Lent, according to the Catholic calendar.

The Venetian carnival, just like the old Roman carnival, meant that for brief period all social inequalities were abandoned: the poor man was as good as the rich, the peasant the equal of the noble; the order was, so to speak, turned upside down. Therefore it was necessary that the mask, hiding identity, be worn. Balls and festivities, held in various squares, were the pulse of the carnival.

The typical garments of the Venetian carnival were the "bauta" (a lace cape and a black silk hood) and the "tabarro" (a large elegant mantle worn with a white mask).

During the carnival, convention was abandoned in the anonymity of it all. Songs, laughter, jokes, libertinism, games, actors, mimicry, itinerant vendors... were everywhere in Venice.

The use of masks (now the most famous in the world) during carnival was reintroduced in 1980. Theatrical performances take place in St. Mark's Square, and, on the last day, there is the traditional burning of the Carnival Puppet. ❯❯

The lagoon and the islands

The lido

The magic of Venice is far from being concentrated in the heart of the city – it extends to the thirty four islets that make up its surroundings.

First the Lido: on its seven kilometres of sandy shores stand the Excelsior Hotel, in pseudo-Oriental style, and the superb recently built Des Bains where Luchino Visconti filmed "Death in Venice". Virtually empty at the beginning of the century, during the two World Wars it became an internationally famous resort.

Today the Film Festival and the Casinò (transferred to Venice during the winter) further attract tourists. At its southern tip is the antique village of Malamocco (the first inhabited place in the lagoon), where the government of Heraclea settled between 700-800 AD before founding Venice. In Malamocco's main square stand an antique church and the palace of the Podestà in Gothic style.

Chioggia

The little town lies on two small parallel islands and the streets are set at right angles. From the Canale della Vena you get to Corso del Popolo with its many arcades where is held the colourful, cheerfully noisy fish market.

Then there is the cathedral reconstructed on a design by Longhena and the Campo del Duomo where rises the small church of San Martino.

Torcello

Torcello was the birthplace of Venice. Seen from the sea are the outlines of its ancient churches. The quiet life of Torcello, it has only about 60 inhabitants, is concentrated in its picturesque little square. And here are the religious origins of Venice. Next to the two small 14th century palaces of the Archives and the Consiglio, stands the religious complex: the remains of the extremely old Baptistery and the Cathedral of Santa Maria Assunta (founded in 639 AD, restructured and enlarged after 1000 AD). The latter has three naves with two rows of nine columns, a marblemosaic pavement, a bishop's throne and a Roman sarcophagus containing the relics of St. Heliodorus. There is also the Church of Santa Fosca built shortly after 1000 AD.

Murano

The boat continues to Murano which consists of five islets. It has been for centuries the centre of the fragile but noble art of glass-making and is still today actively researching original and unusual shapes and techniques. Murano glassware is the most prestigious in the world, with the possible exception of Bohemian glassware.

The religious complex of Santa Maria and San Donato

In the palazzo Giustiniano is the Museum of Venetian Glass where are displayed archaeological finds, great works of the illustrious past and contemporary pieces; they show how the art of glass-making developed from the technique of mosaic cutting in Byzantium, whose influence has always been felt in Venice. In the streets of Murano are the surviving "home-factories", small complexes which comprise the artisans' home and shop.

Do not leave this "island of islands" without looking at the beautiful Palazzo Trevisan and Palazzo da Mula and especially at the religious complex of Santa Maria e San Donato, the loveliest old building on the island. Founded in the 7th century, it was restructured in 1100. It has three naves with marble columns. The mosaic pavement was finished in 1140. Very remarkable is the Madonna against a gold background. The complex is of unique beauty.

Burano

The last stop of our tour of the major islands is to Burano, the home of lace-making. Burano is very old, certainly Roman; after 1000 AD it was already a flourishing town. There are many monasteries on it. The Church of Santa Maria delle Grazie is noteworthy. The remaining sights are concentrated in the main square: they are the ex oratorio di Santa Barbara and the Church of St. Martin. But who could leave Burano without visiting the Scuola-Museo del Merletto which today is a cooperative of lace-makers where more than 70000 products tell the story of 3 centuries of lace-making.

San Lazzaro degli Armeni and other islets

The boat circumnavigating Venice now moves amongst a few small islands, some are real little gems, some show signs of having been abandoned, others maintain the blessed quiet of convents as in San Lazzaro degli Armeni. Here on this tiny green islet the great religious building has endured, unaltered, for nine centuries. You can visit the picture gallery, the museum – one room of which is dedicated to the poet Lord Byron who used to retire here to meditate – and the beautiful library. In the monks' garden peacocks parade vaingloriously. Back on the boat, we are guided through the 34 islets by the "bricole", long poles driven into the sea-bed forming a route for the boats. This time to the island-convent called San Francesco nel deserto (St. Francis in the desert), silent and beautiful. The island was given to the Franciscans in 1228 and they have lived here ever since, except for a brief interval. They own a small church, two silent cloisters, a beautiful garden with its path lined by high cypress trees. All around slender boats float by on the lagoon.

FLORENCE

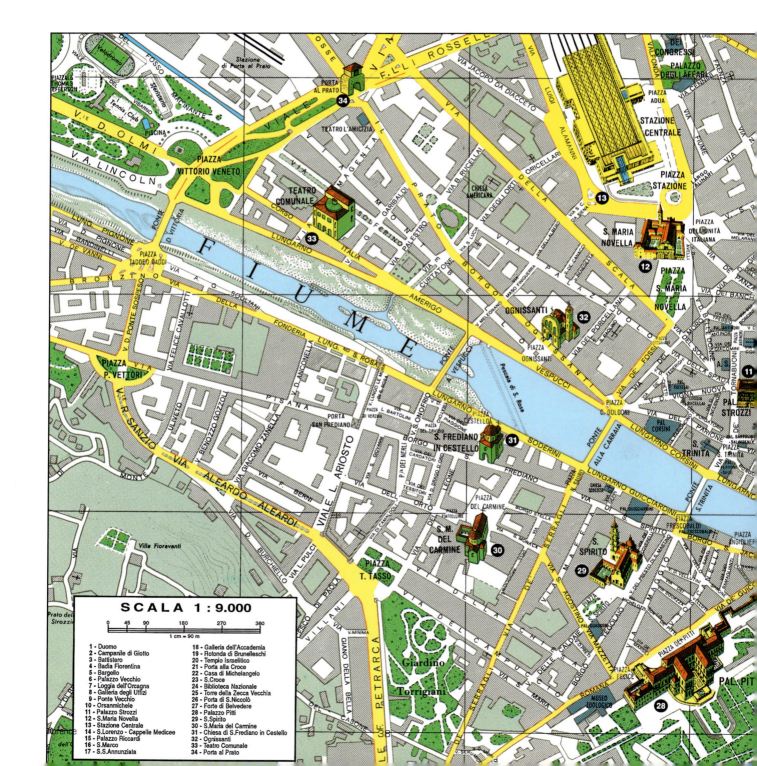

SCALA 1 : 9.000

0   45   90   180   270   360
1 cm = 90 m

1 - Duomo
2 - Campanile di Giotto
3 - Battistero
4 - Badia Fiorentina
5 - Bargello
6 - Palazzo Vecchio
7 - Loggia dell'Orcagna
8 - Galleria degli Uffizi
9 - Ponte Vecchio
10 - Orsanmichele
11 - Palazzo Strozzi
12 - S.Maria Novella
13 - Stazione Centrale
14 - S.Lorenzo - Cappelle Medicee
15 - Palazzo Riccardi
16 - S.Marco
17 - S.S.Annunziata

18 - Galleria dell'Accademia
19 - Rotonda di Brunelleschi
20 - Tempio Israelitico
21 - Porta alla Croce
22 - Casa di Michelangelo
23 - S.Croce
24 - Biblioteca Nazionale
25 - Torre della Zecca Vecchia
26 - Porta di S.Niccolò
27 - Forte di Belvedere
28 - Palazzo Pitti
29 - S.Spirito
30 - S.Maria del Carmine
31 - Chiesa di S.Frediano in Cestello
32 - Ognissanti
33 - Teatro Comunale
34 - Porta al Prato

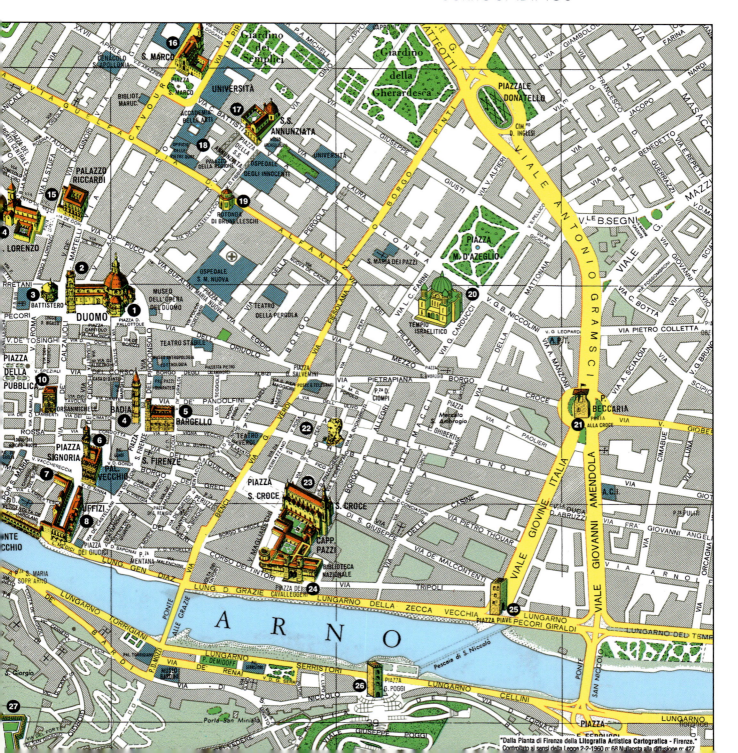

historical background

As ancient Athens and Jerusalem, so Florence was a beacon of civilisation. Rich in works of art, built in a splendid landscape, surrounded by harmoniously rolling hills, Florence for more than a thousand years developed every possible form of political rule: from the supreme power of bishops to the corporate and popular organisation of the guilds; from a true democracy of the people (the Ciompi) to a theocratic republic (Savonarola); from an enlightened absolute monarchy (that of Peter Leopold of Lorraine), from the independent Comune to the Signoria.

Here in Florence power was often closely allied to patronage of the arts, to political theorists (Machiavelli and Guicciardini), to a religious prophetic spirit, to the birth of its language and poetry (Dante and Boccaccio) and to the outpourings of a new artistic vision, from Giotto to Masaccio to Botticelli, to Beato Angelico, from Donatello to Michelangelo. During the Pliocene, present day Tuscany was submerged by the Tyrrhenian Sea which actually lapped the Apennines. But if this late appearance of Tuscany is certain, the origins of Florence is less certain. Some claim Etruscan origins, others, upheld by archaeological evidence, claim it to be of Roman origin, in point of fact to have been founded by Julius Caesar himself. The Roman dictator probably founded it around 59 BC during the April feast of the Floralia (hence the name Florence) in order to give land to his veterans and to pacify the neighbouring towns, including Fiesole, today a flourishing tourist and art centre, then a rich and powerful city which was a positive rival to Rome.

From the 4th to the 9th centuries Florence was conquered by the Barbarians, the Byzantines, the Lombards, and languished until the Carolingian revival. Religious and political struggles tore it apart around 1000 AD, but during these struggles the voice of the nameless masses began to make itself heard in the government of the city: it therefore follows that throughout its future history it was marked by religious motives and by popular excesses. It so happened therefore that under the rule of Countess Matilda, when Florence at the beginning of the 11th century began its territorial expansion, the first seeds of the future Comune were sown, and its commercial activities began to prosper. While Florence was developing its commercial activities, it continued its conquest of the surrounding castles and villages. Thanks to Guelf support, il primo popolo, the working classes, took over power in 1250, but in 1260 Florence knew the bitterness of defeat at the hands of the Ghibelline and Sienese forces at Montaperti. This counterblow led to the abolition of the people's institutions and to the destruction and the 'decapitation' of the towers belonging to Guelf families living in Florence. Later, thanks to French support, the Guelf reassumed their dominion over the city; then it was the turn of the rich merchant families, the popolo grasso, to take the upper hand. Towards the end of the twelfth century, new forms of government were being experimented with until the Ordinamenti di Giustizia (statutes of justice) of Giano della Bella from which the nobility was excluded. But the turmoils did not come to an end: the Guelf faction was internally divided into the bianchi – the Whites – and the neri – the Blacks. Florence expanded further by conquering Pisa and thus obtaining access to the sea. One great family emerged from amongst their rivals: the Medici. Originally from the Mugello valley, the Medici accumulated great wealth during the 14th century thanks to commerce and banking. It was Giovanni di Bicci who emerged as the family founder, firmly assuming its leadership which led slowly to the Medici's political rule of Florence and eventually princely privileges as well. The subtle art of Cosimo the Elder (1389-1464) consisted in never holding any public office in the city, but in becoming its true ruler owing to his allies and his enormous economic power, which he controlled from the splendid Medici palace, designed by Michelozzo in the centre of the city. After Cosimo came Lorenzo, surnamed the Magnificent, who brought the city to the heights of its power owing to his patronage of the arts and to his intelligent foreign policy which earned him the title "pivot of the Italian scale". Under Medici rule, Florence became the major centre of European humanism. In the middle of the 16th century the first signs of a Florentine crisis appeared which would slowly lead to the decline of this city that had been a beacon for the whole of Europe. Commercial restrictions, internal production problems, the imminent epidemic of the pest, commercial competition from northern Europe especially from the wool and textile sector, made life in Florence very difficult under the successive rules of Cosimo the First, Ferdinando the First and Second, and Giangastone,

the last and unfortunate Medici personage whose death without heirs in 1737 ended the Medici dynasty. It fell to the princes of a foreign dynasty, the Lorraine, Franz Stephan and Peter Leopold, to restore political balance, economic equilibrium, just laws and acceptable economic stability. The 17th century in Florentine history is judged to be one of decided decadence, it will nevertheless yield fruits both in the arts and science. It is true that the shades of Michelangelo, Machiavelli and Guicciardini (pioneers of modern political thought) had gone, but Florence still produced a new musical genre, the melodrama, with the "Camerata di Bardi" (1576) , the well known "Accademia della Crusca" founded in 1612 which decided the supremacy of Florentine in the domain of Italian linguistics, and above all it witnessed the exploration of the heavens by Galileo Galilei, the founder of the "experimental method" in science. Let us go back for a moment to Peter Leopold, a great enlightened ruler. During his rule Florence adopted new regulations for the theatre, schools and industry; capital punishment was abolished; furthermore he drafted a new constitution which anticipated the end of absolute monarchy. However, it was never approved. Under his rule Tuscany enjoyed the laws and benefits of a truly modern state. In 1790 he left Florence to ascend the imperial throne in Vienna. Leopold the Second, a kindly drowsy grand-duke nicknamed Hemp, reigned until 1859 when a peaceful revolution compelled him to leave Florence. A plebiscite decided on the annexation of Tuscany by the kingdom of Piedmont Sardinia. Italy became a united kingdom, and in 1865 Florence became its capital for a brief five years. During the first thirty years of this century, Florence became once more the intellectual and literary capital of Italy. This was due to the enthusiasm of magazines, new editors, literary cafés (above all "Le Giubbe Rosse"), poets and writers who were at once faithful to the Tuscan manner but open to new European trends (Soffici, Cecchi, Pallazzeschi, Pratolini). Ottone Rosai turned back to realism in his paintings, which are ever more and more admired for their greatness and originality. During this period Florence tried to revive its economy and tourist trade. It inaugurated the "Maggio Musicale Fiorentino", the "Mostra Internazionale dell'Artigianato" and the building of new works such as the railway-station in Florence and the Church of S. Giovanni Battista on the Autostrada del Sole (Sun Motorway) by Giovanni Michelucci. The city was bombed during the Second World War and all its bridges destroyed by the Germans in flight except for the Ponte Vecchio (the "old bridge"). The Resistance in Florence was strong enough to contribute largely to the hunting down of Fascists and Nazis. However, in 1966 there was a new tragedy: the terrible flooding of the Arno which damaged the artistic heritage and destroyed thousands of artisans' shops.

Piazza del Duomo

In the heart of Florence, the Piazza del Duomo is closely linked to the Piazza San Giovanni and is the city's religious centre just as a few hundred metres from here, in the Piazza della Signoria, the beautiful Palazzo Vecchio is the present seat of the municipality and the civic and political centre. Three monumental buildings stand out in the Piazza del Duomo and are amongst the most beautiful and significant in Italy: the cathedral of Santa Maria dei Fiore crowned by the renowned cupola (dome) of Brunelleschi, the ancient Baptistery and its admirable doors and the elegant bell-tower which together become almost a piece of jewellery. It would be useful, however, first to take a look around in order to admire the elegant Loggia del Bigallo. Built in the mid 14th century probably by Alberto Arnoldi, the Loggia del Bigallo was a place where lost and abandoned children were displayed before being fostered, held by the Confraternity of the Bigallo still to this day devoted to charity. In the small museum are now kept the frescoes that used to adorn the façade of the loggia.

Close by is the seat of the Misericordia founded in the 13th century and today the oldest institution of charity in Florence which now numbers six thousand members and still, centuries later, helps the sick and the needy.

Loggia del Bigallo

The Cathedral

Five hundred metres long and thirty eight metres wide, Santa Maria del Fiore, built on the former ancient Basilica of Santa Reparata is one of the largest religious buildings in the world. Arnolfo di Cambio (from 1294) and Giotto contributed successively to the building, although Giotto was particularly dedicated to work on the bell-tower. In mid-14th century, Francesco Talenti enlarged the structure of the building. Enclosed in an extremely narrow space, the Duomo dazzles us especially by the beauty of its polychrome marble covering (green marble as in the ancient Baptistery, white marble and the red marble from Maremma, all recently restored) and by the imposing elegance of the huge Dome built quite a time after the cathedral by Brunelleschi, on the audacious diameter of forty two metres. The gothic style façade of the cathedral is, however, modern. Like so many Florentine churches, the Cathedral was left without a façade for centuries, although one was started by Arnolfo who sculpted beautiful statues to adorn it. The much talked about actual façade was finally built, thanks to public donations, in 1877 by Emilio de Fabris, winner of the much sought after and discussed competition. The admirable and deliberate sobriety, the almost naked space inside this temple, enormous but

never to excess, overawes and provokes admiration from witnesses of centuries of memorable events like the Council of Florence which united the Orthodox and Roman churches (1439), the Pazzi conspiracy, during which Lorenzo the Magnificent was wounded, the apocalyptic preachings of Savonarola – a reforming monk who was burned at the stake in Piazza Signoria. There are few remaining great works of art in the cathedral. But the space between the massive pillars and the fascinating light which pours through the rose window of the central nave and the narrow lateral windows are in themselves works of art. In the internal façade there is a beautiful polychrome window from a design of Ghiberti and the Prophets by Paolo Uccello on the face of the clock. In the right nave a bust of Giotto by Benedetto da Maiano and the Tabernacle of Nanni di Banco. The octagonal marble choir by Bandinelli with basreliefs of the Apostles and Prophets are also quite beautiful. Above is a wooden Crucifixion by Benedetto da Maiano. Out of historical curiosity you should also see the panel painting of Domenico di Michelino which illustrates Dante, Florence and the Divine Comedy. Exquisitely beautiful are the equestrian portraits of the 'condottieri' of the Florentine republic, John Hawkwood by Paolo Uccello (1436) and Niccolò da Tolentino, inspired by the former, by Andrea del Castagno (1456). Looking down there is the beautiful geometric floor in polychrome marble by Baccio D'Agnolo (early 16th century). The high vault of the dome is frescoed with a Last Judgement (recently restored) by Vasari and Zuccari (end of the 16th century), more grandiose than beautiful. The extraordinary stained glass windows of the drum were executed from cartoons by such great artists as Donatello, Paolo Uccello, Ghiberti and Andrea del Castagno. Not to be missed is the bronze Reliquary urn by Ghiberti with exquisite basreliefs illustrating the Miracle of Saint Zanobi, bishop of Florence, in the act of resuscitating a small child. Of great interest are the two entrances to the Sacristies (the bronze door of the New Sacristy is by Luca della Robbia).

Brunelleschi's Dome

From almost every part of the city and even from beyond it, the one hundred and fourteen meter high dome of Brunelleschi can be seen, the first to be built since antiquity. Although inspired by the Roman Pantheon and colossal in all its structure, it has nevertheless a slim and elegant Gothic grace. It is still today an unexplained feat of Renaissance structural engineering. To the amazement of all, it was built without using a wooden supporting frame to sustain the vault during construction. He used only a building apparatus invented by himself. The dome has two concentric shells. Its base rests on sturdy pilasters around the domed tribunes, soaring upwards by a play of thrust and counter thrust. Brunelleschi conceived this audacious structure as a skeleton consisting of eight main ribs at the corners of an octagon, reinforced by another sixteen lesser ribs, all of which are braced by stone arches. The dome was completed in 1436 and has always inspired admiration.

Giotto's bell-tower

stonetracery

In 1334 when Giotto was appointed to design the bell-tower, the Florentines wanted it to be beautifully and richly adorned. Within barely thirty years it was completed: the richest sculptural undertaking of the early 14th century, an unusual combination of solid Roman classicism and Gothic elegance. Three great artists worked on it: Giotto, who conceived the project and designed the first storey, Andrea Pisano (in 1340) who designed the second storey accentuating its vertical and slender aspect by adding doublearched windows, and finally Francesco Talenti who, by covering the whole with precious marble, transformed it into a gemlike work. The three types of marble are: the white of Carrara, the red of San Giusto and the green of Monte Ferrato. In order to pay for its building, the city of Florence contributed by paying a special tax. The belltower is decorated with basreliefs by Giotto on the first storey, and with sixteen sculptures, mainly by Donatello, now replaced by copies; the originals can be admired in the near-by Museo dell'Opera del Duomo. »

The Baptistery

The oldest and perhaps most beautiful amongst the great Florentine monuments, is the Baptistery, called by Dante his "beautiful St John's". Built on an edifice of the 5th century, thus making it the oldest building on the square, the Baptistery is unrivalled because of the perfect harmony of its proportions, the elegance of its green and white marble covering (in the pure Romanesque style) and for the three sets of bronze doors: two are by Ghiberti, and Michelangelo called the set facing the cathedral the Door of Paradise.

The exquisite tessellated pavement of marble mosaic suggests echoes of pre-Christian or even Etruscan symbology. The interior is decorated by splendid mosaics by Jacopo Francescano, who probably first worked on them (1225), and other Florentine and Venetian artists. Cimabue is also thought to have taken part in the decoration of the vault.

The mosaics, which illustrate scenes from the story of Genesis, are dominated by the huge figure of Christ (8 meters wide) in the Byzantine tradition.

The chief ornaments in this building are the three sets of doors: the south door by Andrea Pisano, the north and east doors by Ghiberti. The east door, later called "of Paradise", took Ghiberti 25 years to complete (it was finished in 1452). The ten panels show scenes from the Old Testament, Adam and Eve, the Story of Noah, Cain and Abel, and the equisite Meeting of Solomon and the Queen of Sheba (bottom right).

The panels, which show narrative unity and an impressive mastery of perspective, are surrounded by an elegant frieze of fruit, foliage and birds. The Doors of Paradise are undoubtedly a masterpiece that attracts admirers from all of the world, especially after restoration has returned the gilding to the surface with spectacular results. What had been first a pagan temple and then the ancient cathedral of the city, was rebuilt in 1128 as a baptistery. This octagonal building is the oldest example of Romanesque architecture in Florence, and became a prototype, especially the use of multicoloured marble inlay, for other Florentine churches such as San Miniato al Monte and the Badia Fiesolana.

Ghiberti
Door of Paradise

Donatello, Choir

Museum of the Opera del Duomo

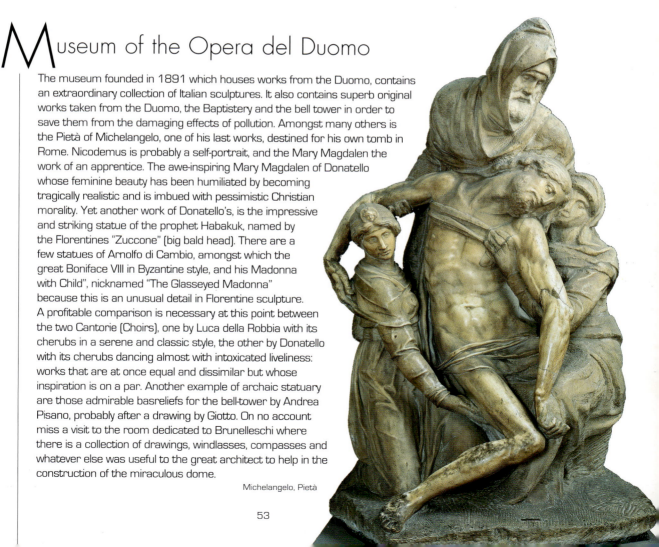

The museum founded in 1891 which houses works from the Duomo, contains an extraordinary collection of Italian sculptures. It also contains superb original works taken from the Duomo, the Baptistery and the bell tower in order to save them from the damaging effects of pollution. Amongst many others is the Pietà of Michelangelo, one of his last works, destined for his own tomb in Rome. Nicodemus is probably a self-portrait, and the Mary Magdalen the work of an apprentice. The awe-inspiring Mary Magdalen of Donatello whose feminine beauty has been humiliated by becoming tragically realistic and is imbued with pessimistic Christian morality. Yet another work of Donatello's, is the impressive and striking statue of the prophet Habakuk, named by the Florentines "Zuccone" (big bald head). There are a few statues of Arnolfo di Cambio, amongst which the great Boniface VIII in Byzantine style, and his Madonna with Child", nicknamed "The Glasseyed Madonna" because this is an unusual detail in Florentine sculpture. A profitable comparison is necessary at this point between the two Cantorie (Choirs), one by Luca della Robbia with its cherubs in a serene and classic style, the other by Donatello with its cherubs dancing almost with intoxicated liveliness: works that are at once equal and dissimilar but whose inspiration is on a par. Another example of archaic statuary are those admirable basreliefs for the bell-tower by Andrea Pisano, probably after a drawing by Giotto. On no account miss a visit to the room dedicated to Brunelleschi where there is a collection of drawings, windlasses, compasses and whatever else was useful to the great architect to help in the construction of the miraculous dome.

Michelangelo, Pietà

Piazza della Signoria

A few hundred metres from the religious centre of Florence, that is to say the cathedral, is the Piazza della Signoria which for eight centuries has been its political and civic centre. First named of the Priori (the magistrates who met in the Palazzo Vecchio), then of the Grand Duke, this square has witnessed the great historical events of Florence. Here worked Niccolò Machiavelli who had a study in the Chancellery of the palace; Pope Leo the 10th passed through it; here the reforming monk Savonarola was burned alive (a porphyry plate in the middle of the square on the ground marks this event); here Bonaparte's troops planted the Tree of Liberty; here was proclaimed the plebiscite announcing the annexation of Tuscany to Italy; here the German dictator Hitler made a speech. Since 1872 Palazzo Vecchio has been the town hall and also the official residence of the Mayor. Dominated by the massive asymmetrical Palazzo Vecchio and by the exquisitely beautiful Loggia della Signoria (also called dei Lanzi, because Cosimo the First's German guards, the Lansquenets, lived here), the Piazza della Signoria contains important works of art: from the equestrian statue of the Grand Duke Cosimo the First of the Medici by Giambologna (1594) to Neptune's fountain by Ammannati with the horses and large white central figure which the Florentines nicknamed Il Biancone (The Big White One), and its elegant bronze female figures. Then there is an important work on the steps of the Palazzo Vecchio: Judith killing Holofernes, a copy of Donatello's original which is kept inside the palace. The copy of Michelangelo's David (the original is in the Accademia Museum and another copy is in the Piazzale Michelangelo) and the imposing group of Hercules and Cacus by Bandinelli (1533) are placed at the top of the steps, thus creating an effective setting. The Loggia della Signoria, also called dei Lanzi, is an incomparable jewel built by Benci di Cione and Simone Talenti around 1380. It is a symbol of democratic Florence because here took place the investiture of the Priori (initially three, then six and eventually twelve, they were supreme magistrates who lived here during their two month tenure of office in the government). Now it is a sort of small precious open-air museum. Here one can admire a few protected masterpieces, amongst which the bronze Perseus (in restoration) by Benvenuto Cellini, the great goldsmith and sculptor. In his famous "Autobiography", he provides a graphic description of the serious difficulties he encountered while casting it. Perseus, the son of Zeus, managed to behead the Medusa, a mythological figure who turned all those who looked at her to stone. Another masterpiece in the loggia is The Rape of the Sabine Giambologna, (1583) a magnificent and elaborate serpentine composition.

Neptune's fountain, the "Biancone" by B. Ammannati

Palazzo Vecchio

This building was erected by Arnolfo di Cambio in 1299. Under the Medici, numerous alterations were made in order to transform the original fortress, built on an antique Ghibelline tower, into a luxurious residence. The Palace was called the "Old Palace" as Cosimo the First in the 16th century left it in favour of a ducal residence in the Palazzo Pitti, which became the "New Palace". At first sight it may seem severe. It is an excellent example of civic Florentine architecture, irregular and asymmetrical with its main doors not placed in the centre, two windows on one side and three on the another. Today it seems more elegant because of the marble two-light mullioned windows, previously in stone, and the 18th century terrace.

The tower, from which one can admire a panoramic view of the city, was built a century later and shows Ghibelline crennelations which is curious considering it was built and commissioned by the Guelfs.

Many artists in varying epochs, as already pointed out, have worked on the Palace. The first courtyard was redesigned by the great Michelozzo at Cosimo the Elder's wish. In the middle of the fountain is a copy of Verrocchio's Winged Putto (Cherub); the original is kept inside. Around the 16th century the columns were covered with elegant stucco work and the walls painted with views of Austrian cities in honour of Joan of Austria, who was married to the Grand Duke Cosimo the First's son, Francesco the First. The monumental grand staircase by Vasari goes to the first floor, to the heart of the Palace which is the Great Hall of the Five Hundred. The monk Savonarola, then the head of the new anti-Medici democratic republic, commissioned Cronaca to build the big Hall destined to hold the meetings of the large Florentine governing assembly which ruled the republic. The work was completed between 1494 and 1496. But with the Medici back in power, the Grand Duke

florence

A. Verrocchio,
fountain in courtyard

Cosimo the First transformed the hall into a room where he gave audience (on one side can be seen the raised platform where Cosimo sat). Cosimo wanted Vasari, the complacent and eloquent proclaimer of the Medici, to fresco a series of large paintings glorifying the Medici fortunes. Due to Vasari's additions and frescoes, the cartoons of the Battle of Anghiari by Leonardo and the Battle of Cascina by Michelangelo were lost forever; in their stead are Vasari's paintings singing the praises of the Medici.

In the 19th century, in this very Hall, the annexation of Tuscany by Italy (1859) was proclaimed and later, when Florence was the capital from 1865 to 1870, it housed the Chamber of Deputies. Quite different in size and inspiration, yet evocative, is Francesco the First's little study, son and heir of Cosimo, who was very unlike his father in his political and military views and preferred the solitary study of alchemy. This tiny narrow study built by Vasari in 1570 has a beautiful barrel vault frescoed with allegorical motifs by Poppi. It is also decorated by meticulous and dazzling portraits of Cosimo and his wife Eleonora of Toledo, works of Bronzino and some paintings by Stradano. There are many large and magnificent rooms to visit on the second storey of the Palazzo Vecchio. The important ones are the Quarters of the Elements, the Room of Cybele, that of Ceres, and the Room of the Sabines with frescoes by various painters of the period: Stradano, Vasari and Bronzino. On no account miss Eleonora's Bedroom, the Room of Justice, the Old Chancellory and the Wardrobe Room.

Great hall of the Five Hundred

The Sala delle Udienze, also called the Room of Justice, is where the monk Savonarola was condemned to death (he was burned alive in the square). The coffered ceilings, rolled in pure gold, are by Benedetto da Maiano. On the walls are frescoes by the Mannerist painter Francesco Salviati.

The Wardrobe Room is also called the Room of the Maps because of its splendid and invaluable fiftythree geographical maps painted by Ignazio Danti, friar and renowned Florentine astronomer. In the middle stands "Great Cosmo", the largest globe of its time, made in 1565.

❮❮ Orsanmichele, faith and power
from granary to church

This high square building, now a church but once a granary, is proof of the power of the Florentine merchants and, because of the statues in their niches on all sides, almost an outdoor museum.

Already a church before 1000 AD, then partly destroyed in mid-13th century, it was completely rebuilt as a store-house in mid-14th century. The upper storeys are used for exhibitions and the loggia has been permanently walled-in. Inside Orsanmichele there is a striking tabernacle, "the most beautiful of all times", as its creator Andrea Orcagna wished it to be. Although a sculpture, it has many of the details of a goldsmith's work. It frames the Madonna of the Graces by Bernardo Daddi, a painting the Florentines greatly cherished. The powerful Florentine guilds commissioned statues representing their patron saints to be placed in the elegant niches along the four sides of the church. Among the famous artists who worked on them are Donatello, Ghiberti, Verrocchio and Nanni di Banco. ❯❯

florence ⚜

The Uffizi

The Uffizi (The Offices) is certainly the oldest and perhaps, with the Louvre, the most important art gallery in the world. It has now been visited for four centuries: a repository of European painting and of its development, it displays unbeatable works of art. There is actually a project for the Grandi Uffizi (The Great Offices) which should enlarge the museum with new rooms in order to hang the thousands of works that are still in storage. The history of this building, which Vasari completed in mid-16th century, is indeed a curious one. By harmonising the monumental courtyard, the square and the street, and dividing the whole space into empty and filled spaces, it creates a harmonious and solemn unity which is enriched by columns, portals, niches, windows and loggias culminating in the final wing overlooking the Arno. Cosimo commissioned

Simone Martini, Annunciation

Paolo Uccello, Battle of San Romano

Giotto, Majesty   Rosso Fiorentino, Angel Musician

Piero della Francesca,
Portraits of Federico di Montefeltro
and his wife Battista Sforza

Leonardo, Annunciation

Filippo Lippi,
Madonna with child

the Uffizi in order to have the magistrates and bureaucracy of the Grand Duchy close to the Palazzo Vecchio. Francesco the First, who succeeded Cosimo, transformed the top storey into a museum. So was born in 1591 the first museum in the world in the modern sense. Little by little the complex was enriched by the addition of the Medici Theatre, where entertainment for the court took place, by the gorgeous Tribune, conceived by Buontalenti, a casket for the rarest treasures of the gallery. It is impossible to catalogue even briefly the treasures of the Uffizi. Here can be traced, documented by its very continuity, the complete history of art during the great centuries, from the 14th to modern times. From the The Madonna and Child by Cimabue, to the Blessed Humility by the Sienese Pietro Lorenzetti, and the Madonna and Child by Duccio da Buoninsegna. From the fundamental role of Giotto, here represented by the Madonna and Child of Ognissanti, to the serene and superbly sinuous Annunciation by Simone Martini. From the Adoration of Gentile da Fabriano, which inaugurates the apotheosis of 15th century painting. The Battle of San Romano by Paolo Uccello, much given to the art of perspective. From the portraits of Federico di Montefeltro and his wife Battista Sforza, by the great Piero della Francesca, to the heights of Botticelli's Birth of Venus and La Primavera (The Spring), symbolic maps of humanistic ideals. From Filippo Lippi's Madonna and Child to the Adoration of the Magi and to the Annunciation of Leonardo da Vinci. From Michelangelo's Tondo Doni, which depicts the Holy Family, first expression of Mannerism, to the serene and classically beautiful Madonna del cardellino (Madonna of the Goldfinch) by Raphael. From the warm and golden luminosity of Titian's Venus of Urbino to Pontormo, neurotic Mannerist genius, with his extraordinary Supper at Emmaus, to Rosso Fiorentino's Angel Musician, to the terrifying and powerful Medusa head by Caravaggio.

Michelangelo,
Tondo Doni

florence

« Botticelli's dream-like "spring"
a timeless myth

"The Spring" is the painting that definitely closes the long middle ages and inaugurates the first part of the Renaissance. Botticelli (1445 to 1550) paints with the refinement worthy of a goldsmith (which he had been) and paints with harmonious forms the world of lay serenity cultivated in the second half of the 15th century at the Florentine court of Lorenzo the Magnificent amongst refined and penetrating intellects as that of Pico della Mirandola and Marsilio Ficino. The "Spring" (commissioned in 1480 by Lorenzo di Pierfrancesco Medici) is a great allegorical mythological painting which invites its beholders to enter into the garden of spring that is to say into the new world of the new man of the Renaissance. The allusions and references of the paintings' complex allegory are not at all clear, even today. Inspired perhaps by a work of the Medici poet Agnolo Poliziano Botticelli places in the centre a young woman who perhaps is representative of Humanity. On the right Zephyr, the God of Winds, is chasing a nymph and has by his side the ravishing Flora. To left the three graces perform a stately dance and Mercury waves away the clouds. The whole composition is pervaded by beauty and elegance, the Graces dance their transparent garments ruffled by the wind, Flora advances slowly, the brilliant landscape: all are a reminder of the secular paradise dreams of by the Humanists. »

The important bridges over the Arno

From the Uffizi, or better still from the Palazzo Vecchio, a passage called Corridoio Vasariano (The Corridor of Vasari), because conceived by Giorgio Vasari, leads to the Pitti Palace. Cosimo the First of the Medici had wished for it in order to reach undisturbed his offices in the Palazzo Vecchio. Today it is a splendid walk and picture gallery which tourists can take crossing the Ponte Vecchio over the Arno. The oldest bridge over the Arno is the Ponte Vecchio. But the most harmonious of the Florentine bridges is the Ponte Santa Trinita. The first wooden bridge was commissioned by the Frescobaldi family in 1258, it collapsed a few years later and was rebuilt in stone but it could not withstand the floods of 1333. Erected again from a design by Taddeo Gaddi with six arches, it was swepped away again in mid-16th century. Then rose the actual bridge (1557) by Bartolomeo Ammannati, perhaps based on a drawing of Michelangelo. It is supremely elegant because of the high flat arches, the sharpness of the piers, the scroll ornaments in marble and the span of the gently curving arches. Whilst restoring the bridge, bombed by the Germans in 1944, it was discovered that these arches are "chain like", that is to say in the shape of the curve of a chain hung from two extreme points. The bridge is adorned with statues of the Four Seasons; after the World War II bombings, the Spring by Francavilla was found headless. In 1961 the head was found in the Arno and put back in its place. The second oldest bridge is the Ponte alla Carraia (1218), reconstructed in the 16th century. The third one is the Ponte alle Grazie, previously called the Rubiconte, after the politician who supervised its construction. It was built to link the districts of Santa Croce and San Niccolò.

⟪ The Ponte Vecchio

The Ponte Vecchio is the oldest and most picturesque of the Florentine bridges (hence its name).
It was built to replace an old Roman footbridge and a bridge later destroyed around 1000 AD Built
according to a plan by Taddeo Gaddi, although some claim it to be by Neri di Fioravanti, the chief
architect of the Signoria, it had originally four turrets at its corners. From its inception it housed
merchants and salesmen beneath the open galleries. Apparently the "beccai", that is to say the
butchers, installed themselves there and filthied it so much that in 1594 the Grand Duke commanded
that only goldsmiths could set up shop there.

As it was then, so is it now: sparkling shops suspended over the river in which are firmly set
the bridge's three slightly flattened powerful round arches. By order of the Grand Duke only one
sanddigger enjoyed the privilege of dredging the river-bed from a boat to recover any remnant of gold
fallen in the river.

During the last war the Germans blew-up all the Florentine bridges; although it had been mined, the
Ponte Vecchio was spared. ⟫

florence

The Pitti Palace

Leaving behind the gold of the Ponte Vecchio, we are going to visit the most imposing palace in Italy, the Pitti Palace. Two visits: the first to the private palace, the second to the museums exhibiting the great art collections. Once the home of the Medici and then of the Lorraine, when Italy was united and Florence was for a short time capital (1865-1871), it became the residence of the court of the Savoy. It continued to be their residence until the end of the Second World War. Since then it has been used for shows and exhibitions. It now houses eight museums.

The royal apartments

More than twenty halls, parlours, rooms and ballrooms, redecorated by the Savoy family in the style in fashion in the years 1865-71, witnessed the most splendid ceremonies. The eye travels over magnificent Gobelins tapestries, Empire furniture, canopies, thrones, inlayed cabinets, Sèvres vases, oriental china, Austrian stoves, brocades, chandeliers... Until we finally reach the admirable Sala Bianca (White Room), so-called because of its white stucco decorations. Famous for its banquets and balls, it was built in the 18th century by Gaspare Maria Paoletti. The stucco work is by the brothers Albertolli of Lugano and the chandeliers are in Venetian glass. We now go to the rich Museo degli Argenti (Silver Museum) After stopping briefly to look at the 18th century frescoes by Giovanni di San Giovanni and Furini, which represent the apotheosis of Lorenzo the Magnificent, we get to the Medici Treasury where precious vases in amethyst, jasper and sardonyx in rare antique settings, constitute Lorenzo's priceless collection. Further along, the church vestments and vessels belonging to Cardinal Leopold and the splendid Florentine "pietra dura" (semi-precious stones and marbles) mosaics, invaluable vases, goblets and glassware in rock-crystal and lapis lazuli designed by Buontalenti and Bylivelt; ivories, ambers, carvings and

cameos, rings in fantastic settings; the jewellery collection of the last of the Medici, the Electress of the Palatinate, containing rare and curious Baroque pearls mounted in gold. We then get to the so-called Treasure of the Bishops of Salzburg, three remarkable rooms, where are exhibited the most bizarre works of jewellery reflecting the period's taste for the exotic, including: the famous double chalice made from an ostrich-egg mounted in silver gilt.

We will continue our exploration of this royal residence of by-gone days, but first let us stop a while in the Museo delle Carrozze (Carriage Museum) on the ground floor of the right wing, which exhibits centuries-old carriages and sedan chairs, indications both of royal etiquette and of the luxurious manner in which princes travelled. The penultimate stage will be a visit to the Galleria del Costume (Costume Museum). Thirteen richly decorated rooms harbour elegant abstract mannequins tracing the history of costume over two centuries, from the 18th century to the 1920's.

Let us finish our tour by visiting the Museo della Porcellana (Porcelain Museum) in the Casino del Cavaliere, where there is a famous rarely-seen display of Italian, Viennese and French porcelain.

Queen's Bed-chamber

《 Two hundred metres of imposing stone
the Pitti Palace

The Pitti Palace was first built as a private home, and became the official residence of the Medici (under Cosimo 1st) and from 1865 (after the unification of Italy) the royal palace of the Savoy dynasty. The original structure was built for Luca Pitti, a wealthy Florentine who, as Machiavelli recalls, intended it to be the largest private home ever constructed. It was designed by the great Filippo Brunelleschi (who built the Cathedral's Dome) but he died before it was started. The central structure of the building was inhabited by the Pitti family from 1450.

At the time, it was 36 metres high and 55 metre wide, now the façade is 205 metres wide. The façade was first enlarged by Ammannati (who built the bridge of Santa Trinita), and enlarged designed the great courtyard. The two "rondòs", or terrace wings, were added at the end of the 18th century. When the Pitti family suffered a number of misfortunes, the palace was sold to the Grand-Duke Cosimo the First of the Medici, who turned it into his private residence. His wife, Eleonora of Toledo commissioned Tribolo to lay out, on the hillside behind the palace, the magnificent Boboli gardens. Cosimo the First commissioned Vasari to build the Vasarian Corridor (linking the palace to the Palazzo Vecchio) as a means of protecting himself from indiscreet eyes and possible attacks. With the death of the last Medici in 1737, the palace became the royal residence of the Grand-Dukes of Lorraine. During the brief period when Florence was the capital of the newly unified kingdom (1864-1871), it became the royal residence of the Savoy family, and then one of their many private homes. 》

Titian, Portrait of a Gentleman

Raphael, "La Velata"

The Palatine Gallery

Raphael, Agnolo Doni

Lofty princely picture gallery packed with masterpieces not hung in chronological order, as modern museums insist on, the Palatine Gallery offers an exceptional and dense harvest of periods and schools, a rich addition to the already seen examples in the Uffizi. Started by Cosimo the Second of the Medici in the early 17th century and constantly added to, the picture gallery was opened to the public by the Lorraine in 1820, and became state property in 1911.

Here we can admire outstanding paintings of the great masters; for example Titian's Portrait of a Lady and Portrait of Aretino and the famous Mary Magdalen.

But above all, here we find Raphael's ability to merge the Florentine predilection for line with the Venetian love for colour, especially in his portraits that light the stylistic path to geniuses such as Leonardo, Raphael himself and Titian.

There are many works of Raphael to admire here, from the extremely famous Fornarina (the beautiful bakeress loved by Raphael), also known as "La Velata" (The Veiled Woman), the Madonna of the Chair, in which the same model may have been used, to the Madonna of the Grand Duke, a work which owes a lot to the art of Perugino and Leonardo.

Raphael also painted a series of outstanding portraits, such as that of Tommaso Inghirami and the double portrait of Agnolo and Maddalena Doni. Bearing these figures in mind, let us turn to other works by Titian, like the disturbing Portrait of a Gentleman with blue eyes.

Other great Italian painters, such as Andrea del Sarto with his Assumption and Annunciation, surround illustrious non-Italian artists. Worthy of admiration are the Equestrian portrait of Philip IV by Velazquez, the Portrait of Cardinal

Raphael,
Madonna della Seggiola

Raphael,
Madonna
of the Grand Duke

Bentivoglio by Van Dyck, the well known Four Philosophers by Rubens. Before concluding your visit, stop to admire the Concert, once attributed to Giorgione (who may have been responsible for the figure on the left) and now thought an early Titian, a mysterious yet deeply evocative painting, clearly blended into a whole simply by the light and air that permeate it.

« The Boboli Gardens

amongst statues, plants and flowers

Florence has a wealth of fabulous gardens, often secret. However, the largest, the noblest and the most beautiful is undoubtedly the Boboli Garden. It was laid out in mid-16th century for the Grand Duchess Eleonora of Toledo, Cosimo the 2nd's wife.
Successive artists worked on it, Tribolo, a pupil of Michelangelo, Bartolomeo Ammannati and Bernardo Buontalenti, the latter the designer of amazing creations using fountains, grottos and greenery. Splendour, space and elegant inventions make the Boboli the most magnificent of Italian Renaissance gardens, where plants of various essences compete with the waters of a hundred fountains.
Groves, terraces, the hazy little island, the admirable grotto of Buontalenti and the large amphitheatre, make a walk through it a constant source of inexhaustible surprises. Guarded by hundreds of statues, some grotesque some realistic, some using a bucolic theme (like the amphitheatre, these are later additions). The Boboli is a typically Italian garden, where art and nature meet (marble, fountains, cypresses and planes) in the spirit of true Mannerism and 17th century Baroque. »

florence

Santa Croce

The Basilica of Santa Croce is, perhaps, the most beautiful Gothic church in Italy. For seven centuries, since the great Arnolfo founded it, it has been a continually renewed artistic workshop: Giotto, Donatello, Canova right until the liberal 18th century which made it a Pantheon to eminent citizens, because here also are the tombs and monuments of Galileo, Machiavelli, Alfieri, Rossini, Michelangelo, Foscolo, Ghiberti and Dante Alighieri.

The most celebrated works in the church are Giotto's frescoes in the Peruzzi chapel, illustrating scenes from the Life of St. Francis. In the Bardi chapel are depicted legends of St. John the Evangelist and St John the Baptist. They were the source of all the future development of European painting.

The Pulpit by Benedetto da Maiano, the charming oval relief of the Madonna and Child by Rossellino, and the Annunciation and Crucifix by Donatello are also admirable.

The ten chapels show the development of 14th century Florentine painting (Maso, Taddeo Gaddi,

Bardi Chapel,
Giotto, Death
of St. Francis

Bernardo Daddi, Giotto). The two exquisite tombs, that of the Humanist Leonardo Bruni by Rossellino and that of Marsuppini by Desiderio da Settignano, are the acme of 15th century sculpture. Next to the church is a charming Cloister. In the Sacristy, damaged by the 1966 flood, hangs the famous Crucifix of Cimabue, recently restored. Beyond the Cloister stands the Pazzi Chapel, one of the most interesting works by Brunelleschi.

Cimabue, Crucifixion

It was commissioned as a chapter house by the Pazzi family in 1430 and was not finished until 1470 after the architect's death.

The 19th century façade of the Basilica overlooks the square, popular heart of the city, where for centuries the Franciscans delivered their sermons.

« The Pazzi Chapel in Santa Croce

marble, stone, reason

In Arnolfo's Cloister, adjoining the Church of Santa Croce, stands the Pazzi chapel, a matchless gem which must be acknowledged as one of the most arresting examples of the serene harmonious style of the Early Florentine Renaissance.

Conceived and partly carried out by Filippo Brunelleschi (the genius who constructed the dome), from 1430 this chapel represents perfectly the architect's innovative vision of a centralised building where harmoniously perfect geometry, the circle and the squareare used to full advantage.

By applying the formula of "divine proportions", and by using grey stone to pronounce the architectural features against the plain white walls, he thereby obtains an effect of the purest harmony.

The whole is surmounted by an elegant dome (as in the old Sacristy of San Lorenzo) embellished by two side arches with circular barrel vaults. »

The church of the Carmine

The Church of the Carmine is in the densely populated district of "Oltrarno" on the other side of the Arno. This church is dedicated to faith but also to art, for here, in the Brancacci chapel, are the frescoes by Masaccio, striking examples of Italian, and European 15th century realism.
The church has but one nave. It was built on the site of an old Romanesque church destroyed by fire and reconstructed in the 18th century by Ruggieri and Mannaioni. After visiting the Sacristy, with polyptychs by Andrea di Lorenzo and Bicci di Lorenzo and crossing the Chapter House (which has an interesting exhibition on how frescoes are painted), we come to the lovely cloister.
But the true interest of the Carmine resides in the Brancacci Chapel, to the right of the transept.

« The Brancacci Chapel

Masaccio's outburst of realism

Masaccio's frescoes in the Cappella Brancacci, shape the form and character of Italian Renaissance painting from its inception.
Giotto's genius anticipated it and Michelangelo reached the peak of its achievements. Massaccio was to influence European painting through the ages.
His greatness resides in his new and brilliant formula "faithful to the vision of truth". The story of St Peter is related in the Cappella Brancacci (later dedicated to the Virgin) by three painters: the elegant and late Gothic Masolino, Masaccio, who worked on it in 1428, just before he died at twentysix, and quite some time later (1490) by Filippino Lippi, a great and subtle psychologist.
By simply comparing the Temptation of Adam and Eve by Masolino with the Expulsion from Paradise of Adam and Eve by Masaccio, the originality of Masaccio's tragic realism is captured. Eve's face is distorted by pain, whilst Adam covers his in shame.
Masaccio's work was immediately understood by his contemporaries to be revolutionary.
The learned use of perspective, narrative unity, the new psychological intensity, the modelling lends to the figures (St. Peter wears an orange cape in all the episodes) and to the whole, a new and solemn beauty. The most arresting fresco is that depicting the Tribute, divided into three scenes.
The Brancacci Chapel was perhaps commissioned by the politician and ambassador Felice Brancacci, member of a wealthy merchant family opposed to the Medici.
The frescoes have recently been restored, revealing new aspects of this incredible cycle. »

Church of Santa Maria Novella

Whilst Santa Croce is the historical seat of the Franciscans, Santa Maria Novella (with San Marco) is the historical seat of the Dominicans, the two dominant religious orders in the city.

It took over a century, from 1246 to 1360, to build this magnificent complex comprising the church, the bell-tower, the cloisters and the graveyard, on what was then still swampy soil. So many historical scenes were enacted here: the Dominicans preached, Saint Catherine proved her innocence before the Inquisition, in the 15th century the famous Council of Florence was held here, and in this church the great theologian St Thomas Aquinas taught.

The superb Gothic façade with Romanesque touches (the use of marble in alternating colours) was completed by Leon Battista Alberti.

Ghirlandaio,
Story of John
the Baptist, detail

Masaccio, Trinity

Spanish Chapel

Next to the stained glass rose window are an old sun gnomon and an equinoctial armilla, works of the astronomer Ignazio Danti.

In here are a number of masterpieces: the sculptures of Bernardo Rossellino, the Pulpit, after a design of Brunelleschi and Masaccio's Trinity. In the side chapels are frescoes by Filippino Lippi, Ghirlandaio and the Strozzi tomb by Benedetto da Maiano. Two important Crucifixes hang in this church: that of Giotto (in the Sacristy), and that of Brunelleschi in the Cappella Gondi. The Green Cloister, with frescoes by Paolo Uccello, is peaceful. The adjoining cloister has an ispiring feeling of harmony whilst in the Spanish Chapel is the glorification of the Dominican order in the famous fresco of Andrea Bonaiuti.

Church of Santa Trinita

Many artists in many epochs worked at embellishing the church of Santa Trinita. It was planned by Neri di Fioravanti in 1250 to be built on an old church site, dating from 1000 AD. A hundred years later the bell-tower was added; the stone Baroque façade is by Bernardo Buontalenti. It was the parish church of various Florentine families, and many artists contributed to its embellishment, amongst whom Neri di Bicci, Spinello Aretino, Lorenzo Monaco and Domenico Ghirlandaio. Study carefully, in the Sassetti Chapel (the Sassetti were rich merchants linked to the Medici), the frescoes by Ghirlandaio illustrating the Stories of St. Francis: among these the Approval of the Order of St. Francis and Saint Francis resuscitates a child. The latter takes place in Florence itself and contains many portraits of famous citizens of the time.

Church of the Santissima Annunziata

This is one of the loveliest squares in Florence, because of the harmonious breadth of the three porticoes that surround it – one designed by Brunelleschi – and the graceful fountains by Pietro Tacca. Here stands the Church of the Santissima Annunziata built in 1250 and modified in the 15th century by Michelozzo. The interior is baroque, and contains the fresco (highly venerated by Florentines), deemed miraculous, of the Annunciation, and also important works of Perugino and Andrea del Castagno. Leon Battista Alberti's semi-spherical dome is remarkable, as are the various cloisters: the Chiostrino dei Voti, from a design by Michelozzo with frescoes by Pontormo and Rosso Fiorentino, and the Cloister of the Dead with frescoes by Poccetti and Andrea del Sarto.

The churches of Brunelleschi

The most complete monuments of the Early Renaissance in Florence, are two churches by Brunelleschi which witness his unique sense of space: San Lorenzo, near the Cathedral, and Santo Spirito, on the other side of the Arno in the line populated district of San Frediano, in the square bearing its name.

Church of Santo Spirito

Brunelleschi built the Church of Santo Spirito in the 15th century. The artist wanted it to face the Arno, but had to give up this idea as there were too many houses and shanties between the church and the river.

It has kept its simple whitewashed 17th century façade, except for the two side scrolls by Brunelleschi.

The true beauty of Santo Spirito resides, however, in its interior, remarkable for its harmonious proportions and use of colour.

Amongst many masterpieces, perhaps the following are the most outstanding: the Madonna with Child surrounded by Saints by Filippino Lippi, the 16th century Jesus expelling the money-changers from the Temple by the great Mannerist painter Stradano, and the 14th century polyptych by Maso di Banco in the right transept. Not to be missed are the two Cloisters (one by Ammannati) and the 14th century Refectory containing works by Orcagna. The beautiful octagonal Sacristy by Giuliano da Sangallo was inspired by Brunelleschi.

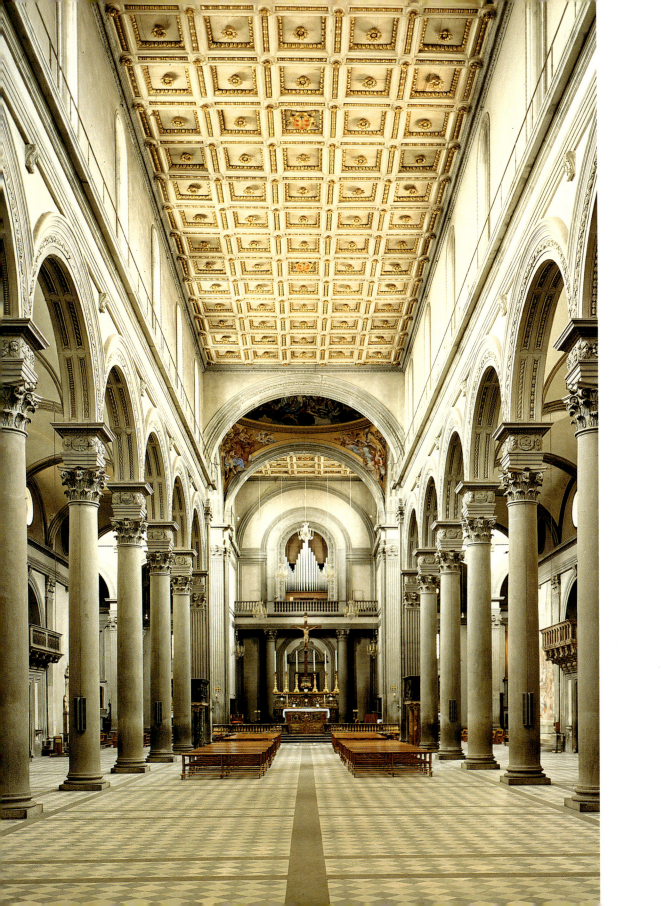

Michelangelo, Tomb of Lorenzo de' Medici

Michelangelo, Tomb of Giuliano de' Medici

Church of San Lorenzo

Both Brunelleschi and Michelangelo helped to renovate the old church of San Lorenzo.
First built in the 5th century and consecrated by St. Ambrose, reconstructed in Romanesque style, it served, for a time, as cathedral of the city; in the 15th century Cosimo the Elder commissioned Brunelleschi to rebuild it.

We owe to the genius of Brunelleschi, and his desire for harmony and serenity, the beautiful serene interior where the use of grey stone contrasts with the pure white plaster walls.

The church contains a unique collection of Renaissance statuary: the Tombstone of Cosimo the Elder, the Tabernacle by Desiderio da Settignano and the two beautiful bronze Pulpits by Donatello, his last work.

The two Sacristies, both the Old and the New, are particularly noteworthy.

The Old Sacristy was designed by Brunelleschi and contains sculptures by Donatello making it a gem of the Early Renaissance. In the porphyry sarcophagus with bronze decorations by Verrocchio rest Pietro and Giovanni dei Medici, the sons of Cosimo the Elder.

In the centre a large marble slab covers the tombs of Giovanni Bicci, founder of the house of Medici, and his wife Piccarda, guarded by a terracotta bust by Donatello.

The New Sacristy, a treasure trove of Michelangelo's works known throughout the world as the Medici Chapels is preceded by the Chapel of the Princes, entirely lined with marble and semiprecious stones; the coat of arms in mosaic are especially notable. The Sarcophagi of the Grand Dukes are by Pietro and Ferdinando Tacca. In the New Sacristy Michelangelo carved the famous Tombs of Giuliano, Duke of Nemours, and of Lorenzo, Duke of Urbino, son and grandson of the Lorenzo the Magnificent. The four great statues (Night and Day, Twilight and Dawn) express the artist's profound meditation on life and death.

Do not leave San Lorenzo without glancing at the extraordinary Laurentian Library and its Vestibule filled with an elaborate staircase in grey stone built after a plan by Michelangelo.

florence

Santa Felicita, Pontormo, Deposition, detail

Other churches

Many other churches in Florence deserve a careful visit. Do not leave Florence without taking a look at the Badia Fiorentina, one of the city's oldest buildings, probably built by Arnolfo di Cambio. Here can be found many different styles, from Romanesque to Baroque. Noteworthy is the Monument to Ugo, Margrave of Tuscany (interesting to note that after centuries a funeral rite is still held here every year). The charming Madonna appearing to St. Bernard by Filippino Lippi and the harmonious Cloister of the Oranges by Rossellino.

Another interesting church is Santa Felicita. The 18th century interior by Ruggieri takes its inspiration from Florentine Renaissance use of greystone.

The superb Deposition by Pontorno is an excellent example of Florentine Mannerism. In this church rests Francesco Guicciardini, the greatest Italian historian of the 16th century. The church was the court chapel of the later Medici and the Lorraine, who could hear mass from the ducal tribune unseen from below.

True music lovers will wish to visit Santa Maria dei Ricci (via del Corso). Although it was built in the 16th century, it has a handsome 17th century portico by Gerardo Silvani. It is famous for its periodic masses in honour of artists, and for its frequent and excellent organ concerts.

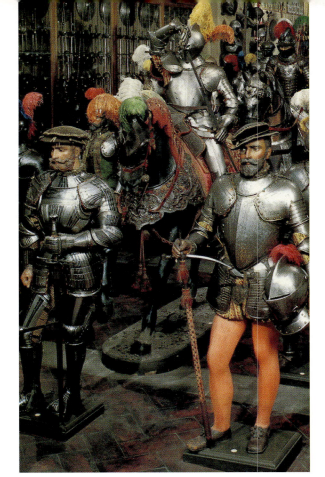

Stibbert Museum

Museums

Florentine museums are countless, as Florence has witnessed centuries of great art.

Let us visit the important ones following an imaginary chronological order. A thorough acquaintance of the treasures of Florence, however, should include a visit to smaller collections such as the Horne Museum, named after the Englishman who founded it at the end of the 19th century, which contains furniture and works of art from the Renaissance onwards; the Bardini Museum founded by Stefano Bardini, famous antiquarian of the last century, which contains furniture and objects from the Middle Ages to the Baroque; the Stibbert Museum displays a rare collection of arms, many of them from the Renaissance.

The Chimera

Archaeological Museum

The 17th century Palazzo della Crocetta (so called because it is in the shape of a cross) near the Piazza della Annunziata, houses a large collection of Etruscan, Egyptian and Greco-Roman works of art. From the Etruscan period there is the famous Chimera, discovered in Arezzo in the 16th century, dating from the 4th century BC, and the Arringatore (the Orator), a significant statue showing the mysterious religious sense of the Etruscans. Another famous and rare work is the Greco-Etruscan François Vase. Cinerary urns, bronzes, sarcophagi and various vessels are of great importance and beauty. From ancient Egypt there are rare finds, mostly taken during Napoleon's wars in Egypt. Here three civilisations from the ancient world can be compared, thanks to the remains that the past has left us.

Beato Angelico, Annunciation

The Convent and Museum of San Marco

The Convent of San Marco, religious centre of the city, where once lived Bishop Antonino (the saint and friend of Cosimo the Elder), Savonarola, Prior of the convent, and the Blessed Fra'Angelico, holds most of the masterpieces of this mystical painter. Here, as we enter the convent and visit the silent cloister, the beautiful Library by Michelozzo (divided into three naves by slim columns), and the narrow austere cells frescoed by the monks, we should be prepared to grasp the religious and prophetic spirit that dominated so frequently the history of Florence. We admire Fra Angelico's spacious simplicity and the use of delicate tints, perhaps influenced by Florentine miniaturists and by the great Masaccio. Among his many paintings: the grandiose Crucifixion, the Last Judgement, the Pala del Bosco ai Frati, the magnificent little panels with the Life of Christ and the Deposition, considered to be his masterpiece. Above all, do not miss his most famous work, the Annunciation, where the peculiar qualities of this holy painter glow in harmonious perfection.

Beato Angelico,
Last Judgement, detail

Ghirlandaio,
The last supper

Michelangelo, Tondo Pitti

The Bargello and the National Museum

Donatello, David

The massive and sombre Bargello – a remarkable example of civic Gothic architecture – prompts the onlooker to thoughts of justice and power throughout history. At once a crucial building of Florentine history and a museum of great works, it is fundamental for the understanding of Renaissance sculpture.

Built in 1255 for the People's Council, it then became the seat of the "Podestà" (the governing magistrate of the city) and of the Captain of the People, called Bargello (hence its name). When Peter Leopold reformed the Civil Code and abolished capital punishment in 1780, the gallows standing in the courtyard was burnt down to the joy of all. For centuries, the Bargello had caused feelings of terror and pity in the hearts of the Florentines.

Today it hosts a great museum. There is a wealth of first class Tuscan statuary, decorative arts, arms and armour, terracottas, reliquaries, crosses, medals, majolicas, furniture, enamels and glassware. The main rooms contain works by Michelangelo, Donatello, Verrocchio and della Robbia. Do not overlook the sculptures by Cellini (Ganymede), by Ammannati (Leda and the Swan), and by Giambologna (Mercury).

The Tondo of the Madonna with Child and a young St.John the Baptist (1504), the bust of Brutus, derived from Roman portrait busts, Bacchus, the artist's first important sculpture, the small figure of David (1531), all by Michelangelo. There are fabulous works of Donatello: the young David in bronze, the Young St. John the Baptist in marble, the St. George holding his shield and the superb relief of the Crucifixion, belonging to his last period. Admirable are the terracotta works of Giovanni, Andrea and Luca della Robbia. By Andrea notice in particular the Bust of a young boy and by Luca the Madonna of the Apple. In the room dedicated to Verrocchio, are displayed his David, his bust of a Lady holding flowers, perhaps a portrait of Lucrezia Donati, loved by Lorenzo the Magnificent. Before leaving the Bargello, pause a while in the evocative courtyard adorned with a large number of coat-of-arms of the former Podestà. Admire the harmonious colonnade, the solemn staircase by Neri di Fioravanti, and the gate by Giuliano da Sangallo.

Michelangelo, Bacco

florence

Della Robbia,
Madonna
of the rose garden

⟪ David, the hero of the Renaissance

masterpiece of Michelangelo

Leonardo's Giaconda and Botticelli's Spring are undisputed masterpieces. And so is David, symbol of Renaissance virile beauty, now become an object of particular devotion by tourists from all over the world. The original is now at the Academy: a bronze copy stands in the Piazzale Michelangelo, and another copy, in marble, stands in front of the Palazzo Vecchio. Until 1872 the original stood in the Piazza della Signoria, symbol of Florentine Republican liberty. Michelangelo was twenty five when, in 1501, he started to work on the David completed by 1505: he worked on a block of discarded marble already roughly carved. The colossal statue is four metres and ten centimetres high. Its symbolic and iconographic characteristics make it a work of striking originality. For the first time, David, the shepherd king, is naked and no longer clad in armour: is portrayed as a man and not a youth, is shown before and not after the combat, and is armed with only a sling (God will give him strength). Originally conceived as a religious work, it was meant to stand outside the Florence Cathedral; only later did it become a political and republican symbol. Probably because the statue was intended to be seen from a distance and foreshortened, unusual details or "mistakes" have been pointed out by art historians: the head and the legs are too slender in proportion to the bust, the right hand is too large and its veins too prominent. ⟫

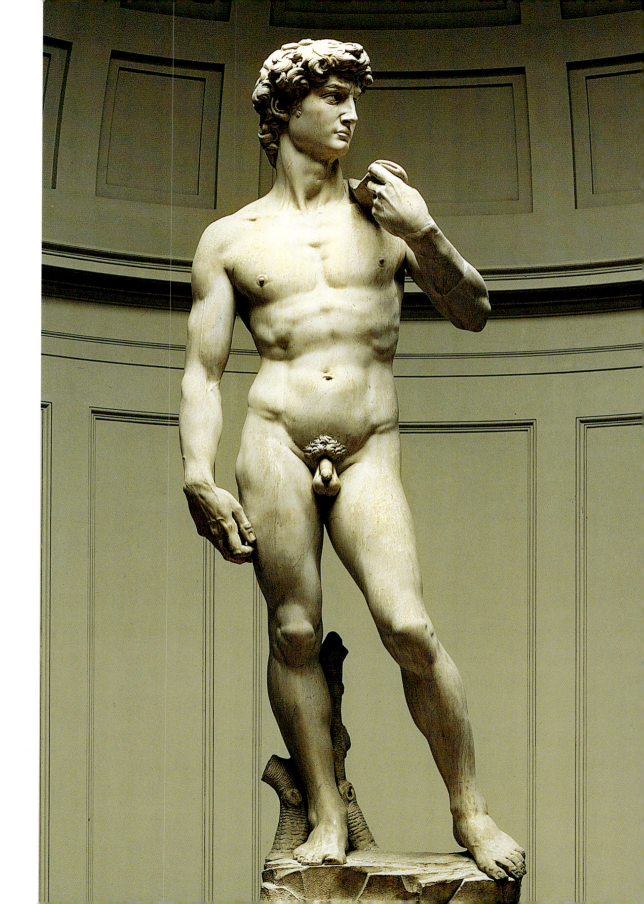

Michelangelo,
Prisoner known
as the bearded slave

Gallery of the Academy

This museum is especially given over to works by Michelangelo. There is not only his David, an exaltation of Renaissance man, but also his Pietà from Palestrina, a masterpiece, certainly, that does not reach the tragic heights of the other Pietà in the Duomo, and the Prisoners, huge and terrible. These last have bodies that seemingly wish to escape from their marble prison in a struggle that is at once physical and spiritual. They were conceived for the tomb of Pope Julius II: Michelangelo worked for almost forty years on this, but it was never completed. The Prisoners are magnificent examples of Michelangelo's so-called "Unfinished Style", that mixes polished and dressed stone, with other parts deliberately left unfinished, still enveloped in the pristine strength of marble. The Prisoners are certainly the most disturbing works of the 16th century in Florence, a century that was to aim at the heroic and modern in Mannerism.

The Academy houses works by important artists wrongly considered secondary by the general public, such as Santi di Tito or Francesco Granacci (end of 15th century): his is The Virgin of the sacred girdle. By Lorenzo Monaco is the superb Christ in pietà and symbols of the passion, a theme still in the Medieval spirit. In order to understand Florentine art it is indispensable to see the superb series of 14th century panels, starting with Nardo di Cione's Trinity.

Michelangelo, Prisoner
known as Atlas

Medici Riccardi Palace, exterior

The palaces

There is a wealth of palaces in Florence: some symbols of the wealth of the merchants, others of political power. The merchants' money could pay for the best architects, which made their homes lasting examples for all.

The Medici Riccardi Palace

Without neglecting other examples of 14th century palaces like the Palagio di Parte Guelfa with its crenellated façade ornamented by a Gothic double-arched window and a picturesque covered staircase that leads to the grandiose Hall by Brunelleschi, or the Palagio dell'Arte della Lana, the old seat of the powerful wool corporation adorned with tabernacles on the façade, let us now visit the Medici Riccardi Palace. It is a remarkably beautiful example of 15th century architecture. It was built for Cosimo the Elder by the great Michelozzo and was the residence of the Medici. The structure consists of a block marked by heavy rustication on the ground floor, contrasting with the lighter simpler plaster work of the top storey. Instead of the old-fashioned crenellations, the building is crowned by a projecting cornice with carved corbels.

Frequent visitors here at the court of Lorenzo the Magnificent were Michelangelo, Pico della Mirandola and Poliziano. In the little private chapel, do not miss the fresco Procession of the Magi to Bethlehem by Benozzo Gozzoli. The Procession of the Magi is an allegory commissioned to Benozzo Gozzoli in 1459 by Piero "the Gouty", to glorify the Medici family. Clad in Eastern costumes (probably copied from those worn by the Greek nobles who participated in the 1439 Council held in Florence) various members of the illustrious family are portrayed. A young Lorenzo the Magnificent is shown on horseback.

Benozzo Gozzoli, Procession of the Magi

The Davanzati Palace

Let us begin with the tall, narrow Davanzati Palace, a unique example of a 14th century luxurious nobleman's house. There are three huge doors on the ground floor, five big windows distributed on three storeys and, at the very top, a loggia rather oddly opening externally, as most loggias gave onto a courtyard. The palace belonged to the Davanzati. Bernardo Davanzati, the great historian, was a member of this family. In the early years of this century, the palace was restored by the great antiquarian Elia Volpi, who recreated perfectly (although not always historically accurate) an example of Florentine life in the Renaissance. It houses the Museum of the Old Florentine House. Large beds, dining tables, "cassoni" and many other furnishings make up the contents of this museum and give a good idea of the home and domestic life of a wealthy Renaissance family.

florence

The Rucellai and Corsini Palaces

We have two more palaces to visit: the elegant Rucellai Palace and the most beautiful private building of the Florentine 17th century, the Corsini Palace. The Rucellai Palace was designed by Leon Battista Alberti and built by Bernardo Rossellino in mid-15th century for the wealthy wool merchant Bernardo Rucellai whose descendants still own and live in the palace. Pilaster-strips and capitals give an impression of elegance and harmony, in contrast to the rustic fortress-like aspect of many Florentine palaces. In the brilliant setting of the Lungarno Corsini, stands

Rucellai Palace

the Corsini Palace. It was ordered by the powerful Corsini family and was designed by Pier Francesco Silvani. Tall, with a charming courtyard and two projecting wings, it catches the eye immediately. The monumental staircase is by Antonio Ferri, the Great Hall enriched with a decorated vault is quite outstanding. On request, the Corsini Collection can be visited. It is a very important private art collection consisting of paintings from the 15th to the 18th century.

The Strozzi Palace

Strozzi versus Medici

The first stone of the Strozzi Palace was laid in 1489 at the order of Filippo Strozzi, then considered "the richest man in the world" and a friend of Lorenzo the Magnificent. However, for many years, the Medici had been hostile to the Strozzi and had them sent into exile. So, as an act of revenge, Filippo wanted a "more beautiful" home than that of the Medici, that is to say the Medici Riccardi Palace in via Cavour. And so it happened that thanks to the spending of hundreds of thousands of florins and to the unusual use of rustication (gradually less pronounced on the 2nd and 3rd storeys) covering the whole façade of this elegant building, a

masterpiece of 15th century Florentine architecture was created. Begun by Benedetto da Maiano (who was inspired by Michelozzo), the building was continued by Giuliamo da Sangallo and Simone del Pollaiolo, also known as "il Cronaca", who designed the elegant projecting cornice, which was left unfinished on one side. The wrought iron lanterns, flag holders and rings (to tie up the horses) were forged by the famous Florentine smith Caparra. It was only twenty years later, in 1504, that the Strozzi family finally went to live in their palace, although Filippo had long been dead. In 1523 work on the trimmings was interrupted, resumed and definitely halted in 1538. At his death in 1913, a Strozzi bequeathed the palace to the State. »

Surroundings

From every part of the city can be admired the beautiful chain of hills embracing the city.

The low, rolling Florentine hills are either covered with vegetation or dotted with villages, creating a mixture of trees and houses, nature and history. The historical villages surrounding the city are easy to reach. It is one of the peculiarities of Florence that the urban centre and the surroundings merge into each other.

From the historical centre of the city, you take a short walk up a narrow winding lane, and you are suddenly in the country, among cypresses, olive trees, villas and old farmhouses.

Still part of the city, yet on the summit of nearby hills, are the following: Villa di Poggio Imperiale; Villa Bellosguardo, dominated by the tower of the same name and once the home of the poet Ugo Foscolo; Pian dei Giullari, where is the Villa il Gioiello, Galileo's last home, and the Observatory of Arcetri, part of the Institute of Astronomy of the University of Florence. Close to the Piazzale Michelangelo is the charming church of San Miniato al Monte. Not far off is the solemn Cemetery delle Porte Sante (of the Holy doors), where lie so many great Florentines.

Panorama of Fiesole

Fiesole

North of the city a long winding road (3 kilometres long), lined with villas and gardens, ascends the hillside to the small town of Fiesole, once a flourishing Roman city even older than Florence. Fiesole was founded by the Etruscans, then became a very important Roman centre. It has two main attractions: the beautiful panorama, the whole of Florence spreads at its feet, and the Etruscan and Roman finds.

Visit: the Archaeological Museum which houses finds from the Bronze Age; the archaeological excavation site; the imposing Roman theatre, which dates from the 1st century AD and seats 3500.

During the summer festival of Estate Fiesolana, concerts, operas, plays and ballet, are performed here.

Halfway down from Fiesole, the small village of San Domenico deserves a visit.

In the church there is a remarkable painting by Beato Angelico: Madonna and Child with Saints. The 15th century Dominican convent is also worth a visit.

On the hill close to Fiesole lies the village Settignano, birthplace of eminent sculptors and skilful stone-cutters. Here Desiderio da Settignano, Rossellino, and Benedetto da Maiano were born. You can visit the pretty cemetery where lie Niccolò Tommaseo and the writer Aldo Palazzeschi.

Then taking via Rossellino through olive groves and cypresses, you reach the Villa Gamberaia (Rossellino) and with a little luck you can visit its admirable Italian gardens.

If you have the time, there are other delightful excursions in store: to the outstanding Medici villas scattered on the hill-sides. Three of them are close to the city: Careggi, enlarged by Michelozzo, lived in by Cosimo the Elder and Lorenzo the Magnificent, is notable for its gardens; Petraia and Castello. Castello was originally a 13th century castle and was transformed and lived in by the Grand Duke Cosimo I.

Abbey Fiesolana

Tribolo, laid out the famous garden with box-hedges, lemon trees, water-sprouts and a large fountain. It is now the seat of the Accademia della Crusca (founded in the 16th century, it studies the Italian language). These perfectly proportioned buildings express the balance between active and contemplative life, between intellect and nature, which was typical of the great Florentine humanists (above all Lorenzo the Magnificent).

≪ Piazzale Michelangelo

Florence at your feet

In 1865, Florence became, for a short time, the capital of Italy. Guiseppe Poggi, the architect, was given the task of adapting the small city for its new role as capital. And so, Poggi had new

ring-roads laid out, following the traces of the old city walls that had been pulled down, in the manner of the Parisian boulevards. Then he had the idea of building on the hillside a magnificent winding avenue (eight kilometres long), which still bears the name "Il Viale dei Colli" (boulevard of the hills). At the end of it he had a square built and named it after Michelangelo. Many Florentines, it appears, "were displeased at the enormous amount spent on it" but the Piazzale Michelangelo offers one of the most beautiful panoramas in Europe. It looks down onto the Arno and its bridges; on the left the view includes the large 19th century Cascine Parks, lower down, the districts of Santo Spirito and San Frediano, to the right the white basilica of San Miniato. The square was the fashionable meeting place for the 19th century upper middle classes. In the centre is a copy

of Michelangelo's David, at its feet four bronze copies of the statues that decorate the Medici tombs in San Lorenzo. If you happen to be here in the right season, do not miss the nearby Iris Garden where these flowers are grown. ≫

Basilica of San Miniato

faith and marble

San Miniato, perched on the hill of the same name, is probably the most beautiful and most perfect Romanesque church in Florence. It is held that a chapel stood here at the end of the 4th century; later, around 1000 AD, a monastery was built here. The present church was constructed in 1207.

The centre of Florence remained pagan. The first conversions to Christianity took place on the other side of the Arno by the legendary St. Minias. Some say he was an Armenian king, others a humble Florentine who was martyred during the persecutions of the Emperor Decius. The façade in green and white marble is astonishingly beautiful.

The sense of balance is perfect, even in the marble intarsia panels of the central pavement, rich in Zodiacal and theological symbols. This church certainly bewitched Alberti, who used some of its motifs for the façade of Santa Maria Novella.

Inside notice the marble chapel by Michelozzo, and the tomb of cardinal Jacopo di Lusitania: behind a delicately sculptured curtain is a harmonious sculpture of Antonio Rossellino (1473).

The Certosa

two encounters: mysticism and art

The Monastery of Certosa, overlooking Galluzzo, two kilometres from Porta Romana, was founded in 1310 by Niccolò Acciaiuoli, diplomat and a member of an influential Florentine family. Certosa, built on top of a hill, has an unprecedented plan. It is inhabited by Benedictine monks. The pious atmosphere and the cells, the silent cloisters and tiny cemetery, all make for a rare feeling of peaceful meditation. The main attraction of the complex is a cycle of five great frescoes (especially the Deposition) by the great Mannerist painter Pontormo; the frescoes were recently detached and restored. A classical painter, Pontormo was forced to leave the city in 1524 because of an outbreak of the plague. He fled, as it happens, to this very Certosa where he studied and was much struck by Durer's etchings. The result was a radical change in his style of painting. The Passion Cycle reflects the influence of German vigour in contrast to Italian harmony. It is not surprising that this pictorial turnabout took place in the heat of the Lutheran Reformation, while Adrian IV of Utrecht was Pope. The end of Italian political and artistic supremacy is nearing. You really should see therefore these masterpieces of Pontormo, which signal the passage from Michelangelo's heights to the atypical manner of 17th Florentine painting, only recently rediscovered by art critics.

florence

ROME

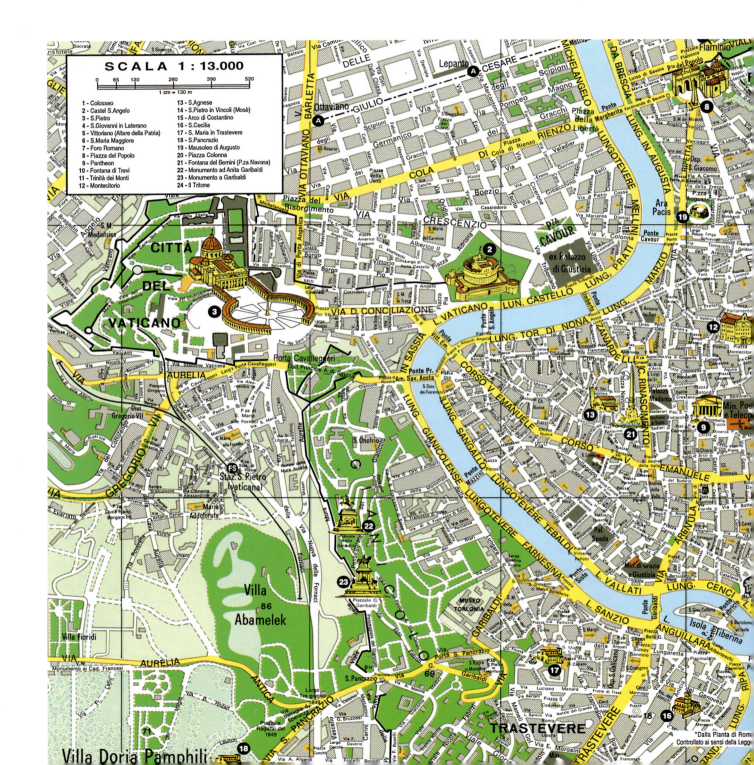

SCALA 1 : 13.000

0 65 130 260 390 520

1 cm = 130 m

1 - Colosseo	13 - S.Agnese
2 - Castel S.Angelo	14 - S.Pietro in Vincoli (Mosè)
3 - S.Pietro	15 - Arco di Costantino
4 - S.Giovanni in Laterano	16 - S.Cecilia
5 - Vittoriano (Altare della Patria)	17 - S. Maria in Trastevere
6 - S.Maria Maggiore	18 - S.Pancrazio
7 - Foro Romano	19 - Mausoleo di Augusto
8 - Piazza del Popolo	20 - Piazza Colonna
9 - Pantheon	21 - Fontana del Bernini (P.za Navona)
10 - Fontana di Trevi	22 - Monumento ad Anita Garibaldi
11 - Trinità dei Monti	23 - Monumento a Garibaldi
12 - Montecitorio	24 - Il Tritone

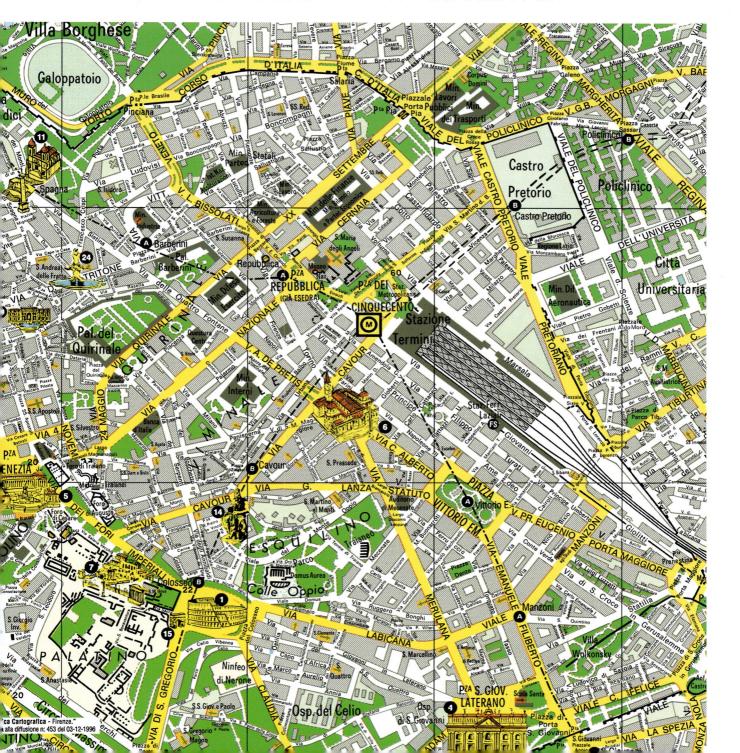

historical background

The history of Rome goes back about three thousand years. It is one of the oldest and most important cities in the world. Latin, which has its origins in Rome, has dominated culture for two thousand years; law, born in Rome, has inspir-ed Western law codes; art and Roman architectural styles have been used as models for centuries in the most advanced countries. The influence of this city, first as the centre of the Roman Empire, then as the centre of Christianity, has no equal in the history of the Western world.

Its beginnings, however, are mysterious. Its very name is an enigma: does it derive from "stroma" (city of the river), from "ruma" (an Etruscan name), or from the legendary Romulus, who might have founded the city with his brother Remus?

This much is certain: Rome originated on the Palatine Hill as a village of shepherds and farmers, and entered history around 753 BC, the traditional date of its founding. At first it was governed by seven kings: Romans and Sabines intermingled and for a few centuries the city was dominated by its neighbours, the mysterious Etruscans. The Etruscans were later chased from the city and in 509 BC the city became a Republic governed by two consuls. At first aristocratic, Republican Rome adopted a harsh form of democracy and established in 494 BC the Tribune of the People, who defend-ed the people against abuse at the hands of those holding power. In the meantime, Rome's political importance was increasing. By 270 BC virtually the whole of Italy was under Roman dominion which very quickly extended its power beyond the boundaries of the peninsula until it became a huge empire.

Under Augustus, the first emperor, imperial Rome reached its zenith, after which started a slow decadence: corrupt emperors (Nero, Caligula, Claudius), the spread of Christianity, the very size of the Empire, the enormous costs of the armies, the pressure of the barbarians along its frontiers.

In 313 AD Constantine acknowledged Christianity as a valid religion and Theodosius in 380 AD proclaimed it as the one and only religion of the Empire. Now the barbarians were closing in: first Alaric then Attila ransacked Rome which consequently was reduced to a minor city in the eastern Byzantine empire. By installing himself in St. Peter's See, the increasingly powerful Pope made Rome the centre of Christianity.

In 800 AD when the Pope crowned Charlemagne emperor of the Holy Roman Empire, it seemed as though the old grand-eur was revived again. It was an illusion. Rome was to witness the long struggle between the papacy and the feudal nobles, and above all between the Pope and the Emperor (struggle for investiture) which gave her historical importance but also left her weakened.

In 1305 the Pope was forced to transfer the papal seat of Christianity to Avignon where it remained until 1367. There now followed two difficult centuries (until the imperial sack of Rome in 1527), but meanwhile the papacy was growing in power and splendour both in art and culture. Popes such as Julius II and Leo X created the great Renaissance and Baroque Rome by commissioning monuments and works of art of unusual splendour to artists such as Michelangelo, Bramante, Raphael and Cellini. The architects Bernini and Borromini built splendid palaces and churches in response to the Protestant Reformation. Baroque Rome with its fountains, gardens and palaces, is one of the highlights of Western culture. Now begins a new age: at the end of the 18th century the influence of the French Revolution made itself felt; Pius VI was deported to France and the short-lived Roman Republic was established. After the Restoration, Napoleon weakened the papacy. It resurged under Pius VII who regained temporal power. Because of the Risorgimento, the Pope was once more forced to flee, and the Republic of the Mazzinian Triumvirate was established. On the 20th of September Italian troops entered Rome, thus putting an end to the temporal power of the Pope and Rome became the new capital of Italy. For half a century there was a cold war between the papacy and the Italian state, ending with the Lateran Pact in 1929 by which date Fascism had taken over. The Pope is now once more the head of Christianity and the head of the smallest state in the world: the Vatican City. Mussolini's Fascist rule tried to bring back to Rome the glories of its an-tique splendours by demolishing edifices, building avenues, stadiums and monuments. The war, the invasion of Rome by the Germans, the heroic resistance of the Romans and the end of the monarchy, mark the birth of the new Italian Republic. After World War II, Rome has seen urban growth, increase in population and the years of the "Dolce Vita" when Rome was capital of the world-renowned Italian cinema.

The places that the world remembers

The Roman Forum

We are in the centre of ancient Rome. Here, Rome builtafter having dried up the marshlandsits Forum where all the political, religious and commercial activities were held, between the Palatine, the Capitol and the Esquiline hills.

It is not easy to move about these ruins without having some knowledge of the ten centuries of history - from the 6th century BC to the Byzantine age - only then, the monuments become meaningful. From the archaic Lapis Niger (Black Stone) to the Column of Phocas - the last monument to be built in the Forum - dating from 608 AD placed in order to celebrate the Byzantine Emperor Phocas. The orators spoke from the Rostra, where all official communications were published. The Curia, the Senate-houses and the political centre of ancient Rome, seems to have been built for the first time by Tullus Hostilius. It was reconstructed in 52 BC, but a new one was inaugurated in 29 BC by Augustus. What we see today is the last reconstruction wanted by Diocletian in 303 AD. The Curia has a magnificent interior although the present wooden ceiling is modern. It was able to seat 300 senators. In the Curia the so-called Plutei of Trajan are exhibited. They are two marble sculptured balustrades that probably decorated the Rostra and emphasised the merits of the Emperor Trajan. They also show how the Forum was laid out at the time.

Basilica Giulia

If the Curia was the political centre of Rome, the Basilica was the place where justice was adminis-trated. The typical basilica was a great rectangular room with arcades on its sides. The Basilica Emilia is the most ancient basilica and the only one of which we have remains. It was founded in 179 BC by the censor Aemilius Lepidus. It looks onto the Via Sacra and was originally richly decorated, but during the Middle Age, it was ransacked by the barbarians. Thanks to archaeological excavations a marble frieze of great interest for the understanding of the origins of Rome was found here. The Basilica Giulia , built by Caesar, was also completely destroyed. The Maxentius Basilica has three aisles and is supported by massive walls instead of the usual colonnade.

After the Curia and the Basilica the temple was the most important building of the Forum. The remains of the Temple of Vesta from the end of the 2nd century BC, are entirely in brick, as is the nearby House of the Vestals; the latter is a large rectangular atrium arranged

House of the Vestals and Temple of the Dioscuri

around a spacious courtyard. Inside the round temple dedicated to Vesta was kept the sacred fire, symbol of the inextinguishable state. In the Forum, there are the remains of the Temple of the Dioscuri, the mythical brothers Castor and Pollux, winners of the battle against the Etruscans and Latins. The temple was built in 484 BC, and then reconstructed in 117 BC, but the only three remaining pillars belong to the reconstruction done at the time of Tiberius. The Temple of Saturn is amongst the most ancient in Rome and is found at the foot of the Capitoline Hills. Its use was to keep the Public Treasury of the city. Further ahead, are the remains of a colonnade that was found a century ago, the so-call-ed Portico of the Dei Consentes. Probably the temple was dedicated to the twelve great divinities of Olympus; inside were kept golden statues of the gods and therefore the building is consider-ed to have been the Roman version of the Greek Pantheon. The Temple of Concord is also found in the Forum. It is an important monument built in 367 BC by Furius Camillus in order to celebrate the end

rome

Temple of Saturn

Temple of Antoninus
and Faustina

of the struggles between the patricians and the plebeians; the podium has been restored many times.

After Caesar was assassinated, his body was cremated in the Forum and a pillar was built in memory of him. In 29 BC a Temple was dedicated to Caesar by Augustus, the first example of the deification of an Emperor. Today there are some remains of the podium and of the tribune in front of it. The Temple of Antoninus and Faustina was dedicated, in 141 AD, by Antonius Pius to his wife, and, after her death, to her imperial memory. It is one of the best preserved temples thanks to the fact that it was converted into a church (now the Church of San Lorenzo in Miranda). Placed on a high podium, it has a splendid façade with marble columns and steps.

The well preserved frieze decorated with decorative motifs is lovely. Unusual is the bronze door kept in the Temple of Romolus. It was built on the Via Sacra (Holy Road) by Maxentius to honour his son who died in 309. It has an innovative structure; a circular building flanked by two rectangular rooms with apses. In the 4th century, Pope Felix IV adapted it as an atrium of the Church of Saints Cosmas and Damian. After the ancient Roman Forum it is worth visiting the later Forums, built during the era of the Emperors and therefore called Imperial Forums.

« The arches of Constantine, Settimus Severus and Titus:

when the emperor celebrated his triumphs

The arch, built as a memorial or to celebrate a triumph, is one of the great inventions of Roman architecture; Rome has many of them.

The most recent, majestic and well preserved is the Arch of Constantine near the Coliseum. It was inaugurated in 315 AD in celebration of the Emperor's victories over Maxentius. However, there are few traces of the Christian Emperor; no signs of his religion, for example, and few references to his life and deeds.

The arch depicts primarily events from the life of the Emperor Marcus Aurelius, soldier and philosopher, because late Imperial artists used sculptural fragments and friezes from older Roman monuments.

Some of the reliefs come from the frieze of a monument celebrating Trajan's victory over the Dacians. The seven medallions on the north and south façades belonged to a pre-existent Arch dedicated to Hadrian. The statues of the eight Dacian prisoners were taken from the Trajan Forum. In the Roman Forum is the Arch of the Emperor Septimius Severus, built in 203 AD., and also dedicated to his children Caracalla and Geta (the name of the last was erased after Caracalla had him killed).

The Arch of Titus is simpler but more elegant; famous is the splendid internal relief showing the triumphal procession bringing the spoils from defeated Jerusalem, which include the altar of the holy temple and the seven-branched golden candlestick. The arch was built in 81 AD. »

rome

The Coliseum:

for the glory of the emperor and the pleasure of the people

The Coliseum is the most beautiful and majestic amphitheatre of Roman times. Its original name, Flavian Amphitheatre, commemorated the name of Vespasian who commissioned the building in 72 AD and inaugurated it by sacrificing 5000 animals. At least until 523 AD (under Theodosius's reign), fights between gladiators and wild beasts were held here periodically. There is no historical evidence that Christians were martyred in the arena. Later the amphitheatre was consecrated to the Christian martyrs and this saved it from destruction, even if many stones of the façade were used for the construction of Saint Peter's. The ellipse of the Coliseum is a magnificent work of architectural engineering. Its measurements are: 188 metres on the greater axis and 150 metres on the minor axis. The façade is 48.5 metres high. The 80 arches serv-ed as an entrance to the 55000 spectators it could accommodate. The exterior travertine covered wall is divided by three orders of engaged columns: Doric (on the ground storey), Ionic (in the middle) and Corinthian. The so-called velarium, or awning, was placed (held by poles and ropes) over the top of the building, to shelter the spectators. Elephants, lions, hippopotamuses but most of all, men, that is gladiators (chosen among slaves, prisoners or criminals), fought and died here for the vile joy of the common people. »

rome

The Imperial Fora

Many other Fora were built when the Roman Forum became too small for the ever increasing Roman population. Today, they are called Imperial Fora.
Many of these Fora are now in ruins because during the Middle Ages they were used as quarries, using the old stones to build new buildings.
Today, if you walk from the Piazza Venezia towards the Coliseum, along the via dei Fori Imperiali, (see chapter on Rome and Fascism), you can imagine what Rome must have been like under the rule of the Emperors.
The Forum of Trajan was the last to be built; it is the most la-vish and was constructed to celebrate the victory over the Dacians. The work of Apollodorus of Damascus, it is 300 metres long and 185 metres wide.
The Basilica Ulpia was built here and now only four rows of columns in the central part are standing. The Forum contained the famous Trajan Pillar which stood between the two libraries and near the Temple of the Divine Trajan.
The Markets of Trajan are a wide exedra made of two semicircular floors with many shops, even on the terraces that crown the building. It is considered the most ancient Roman commercial centre remaining.
Further on, we find the Forum of Caesar which was the first Imperial Forum, inaugurated in 46 B.C. At its entrance is a bronze statue of the dictator.
The Temple of Venus Genitrix was built here; only three columns on the high plinth are still standing.

Forum of Trajan

The Forum of Caesar was built to replace the old Roman Forum and to commemorate Caesar's victory at Pharsalus.

The Forum of Augustus was built in 42 AD as a commemoration of the Battle of Philippi. It is on the other side of via dei Fori Imperiali. Augustus built the Temple of Mars Ultor which is dedicated to revenging mars; there remains today the podium, a few columns, and parts of the colonnade and exedra. The Casa dei Cavalieri di Rodi was built during the Middle Ages and has a well-preserved colonnaded atrium.

There follows the remains of the Forum of Nerva in which are the so-called "colonnacce", two huge columns sustaining an entablature decorated with an elegant frieze dedicated to feminine activities. A massive basement is all that remains of the Temple of Minerva.

A little further on are the ruins of the Forum of Vespasian.

After visiting the Museum of the Fora, located in a nearby convent, to the right can be admired the ruins of the Basilica of Maxentius is a large building from the 4th century AD of which only the original aisles remain. Its vaults are 25 metres high, but the highest ones (53 metres high) have collapsed. Maxentius commissioned it but it was actually finished by Constantine. During the summertime, the Basilica hosts great musical performances. This concludes our visit to imperial Rome.

❮ The Trajan Pillar:
like a film, the glories of ancient Rome

Perhaps, it is the most distinctive among the ancient Roman works of art. It is a story told through photograms (anticipating the advent of cinema). A spiral frieze that turns twenty-three times along the pillar's frame, and that can be read from bottom to top, from left to right. The Trajan Pillar was once multicoloured and is composed of seventeen blocks of lunian marble. It is forty metres high and was erected in 113 AD by the Emperor Trajan in order to celebrate his wars against the Dacians. The forty-five small windows brighten the inside where is a spiral staircase not accessible to the gener-al public. On the top, there was a statue of Trajan but in 1587, Pope Sixtus V replaced it with one representing Saint Peter. ❯❯

Famous roads and squares

A journey to one of the most famous places in Rome can only start from the solemn Capitol, where was once the acropolis (the religious and political centre of ancient Rome).

After the dark years, the Capitol was used as a prison during the Middle Ages. Later, thanks to Pope Paul III, in 1536 this square was entrusted to Michelangelo who designed its structure. After the death of the artist, the square was continued by Giacomo Della Porta and Girolamo Rainaldi. Three palaces mark its borderlines: Palazzo Senatorio, Palazzo Nuovo and Palazzo dei Conservatori; their façades are both harmonious and symmetrical thanks to the balustrades with statues placed over the cornices.

The geometrical quality of the square (one of the clearest spatial solutions of the Renaissance) was emphasised by the great equestrian statue of the Emperor Marcus Aurelius, while the original, after lengthy restoration, is now in the Capitoline Museums, a copy has been placed (1997) in order not to leave the square without a fundamental reference point.

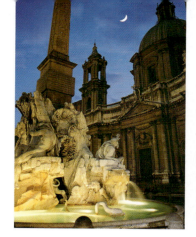

The three fountains of Piazza Navona

The Fountains of Rome:

the fountains that brighten the squares and gardens

Besides the great exuberant fountains, there are many secret fountains in courtyards and also small fountains at the corners of streets (especially in Trastevere) where the water spouts from lions' mouths and from "mascheroni", grotesque stone masks. It seems that the ancient city had two hundred and twelve fountains. The modern ones are for the most part Baroque. After the Fountains in Piazza Navona (see the description of the square), the most magnificent is the Fountain of Trevi; in the centre is Neptune's chariot shaped like a shell, drawn by sea horses led by tritons. This exuberant work of art was done by Nicola Salvi in the mid-18th century in the place where ended the ancient aqueduct of Acqua Virgo. The fountain has become famous be-cause of the film "La Dolce Vita" in which Anita Ekberg bathes in it. It is said that whoever throws in a coin with his back turned to the fountain will one day return to Rome. Another well-known fountain, at the foot of the steps of Trinità dei Monti, is the so-called Fountain of the Barcaccia because it is shaped like a half-immersed boat. It was commissioned by Pope Urban VIII at the beginning of the 17th century and carried out by Bernini or, perhaps, his son Gian Lorenzo. The most elegant of all Roman fountains is that of the Tartarughe (Tortoises) in Piazza Mattei. It was built at the end of the 16th century on a design by Giacomo Della Porta. The four bronze figures of standing youths, a foot on the head of their leading dolphin are splendidly cast by Taddeo Landini. The tortoises were added a century later. The Fontana del Tritone executed by Bernini for Pope Urban VIII in mid-17th century, stands in Piazza Barberini. Four Tritons blow water through a shell held in their hands. Do not miss the fountains in Piazza del Popolo, the two fountains in St. Peter's Square and that of the Naiads in Piazza della Repubblica. However, the list of fountains is never ending. »

Fountain of Trevi

Fountain of the Barcaccia, Piazza di Spagna

rome

Piazza di Spagna and Trinità dei Monti

A church, a flight of steps and a fountain form the most elegant and complex Roman urban site of the 18th century. The Church of Trinità dei Monti was started in 1502 and consecrated eighty years later, at the wish of the French kings who dedicated it to a saint dear to them, Saint Francis of Paola. Inside the church are many chapels belonging to noble Roman families. Notice the double ramp staircase and the twin belltowers.

At the beginning of the 17th century, Pietro Bernini, father of the famous Gian Lorenzo, built for Pope Urban VIII the unusual boat-shaped fountain. A century later, the third marvel was built to connect these two works of art: the Staircase of the Trinità dei Monti, a wonderful Baroque creation. Built in 1723-1726 by the architect Francesco De Santis, it consists of a succession of ramps each made up of twelve steps (total of a hundred and thirty eight steps).

Piazza del Popolo

There are two identical churches and an obelisk: this is the Piazza del Popolo, the apex of the so-called trident because from here ori-ginates - long and straight - via del Babuino, where are many antique shops, which leads to Piazza di Spagna (flanked by via Margutta, a street famous for its painters); via di Ripetta and the very busy via del Corso (Stendhal defined it as "the most beautiful of the world"). Through the Porta del Popolo with its triumphal arch opening into the Aurelian walls, you get the impression, as you enter the square, that you are on the threshold of the most scenographic entrance to Rome. The square slowly took its present shape through the centuries. Pope Sixtus V in 1589 had the obelisk erected at the centre. A century later Pope Alexander VII commissioned Rainaldi to build the twin symmetrical churches of Santa Maria di Montesanto and Santa Maria dei Miracoli (of the Miracles). Because the space on the left was narrower, Rainaldi built a circular dome (for Santa Maria dei Miracoli) and an oval dome for the other church. But they seem the same when you look at them from the square.

The Piazza del Popolo got its larger oval shape in the 19th cent-ury thanks to the gifted architect Giuseppe Valadier, creator of the splendid gardens of the Pincio (which are slightly higher compar-ed to the square).

Piazza Navona

Piazza Navona is a jewel of the Roman Baroque. Its name probably derives from "agone" ("nagone", "navone") that is to say "gara, gioco" ("race, game") referring to the naval battles that took place when the square had a concave bottom which was artificially flooded for naval games. The beautifully shaped square was built on the site of the Stadium of Domitian, of which it has kept the form.

The two greatest Baroque geniuses meet in Piazza Navona: Gian Lorenzo Bernini, creator of the Fountain of the Rivers (the Ganges, Nile, Danube and Plate), and Francesco Borromini, architect of the Church of Sant'Agnese in Agone, unusual because of its splendid concave façade (inside, a 17th century innovation: over the altars, instead of paintings, there are a series of marble bas-reliefs).

Caravaggio,
St. Matthew
and the Angel

Besides the other two other fountains, that of Neptune and that of the Moro (Moor), splendid palaces adorn the square: the Palazzo Pamphilj, planned by the Roman architect Girolamo Rainaldi for the Pamphilj family, patron of the entire square, and in one corner the Palazzo Braschi, built at the end of the 18th century by Cosimo Morelli. The oldest building in the square is the Church of Nostra Signora del Sacro Cuore in front of the Palazzo Pamphilj. It is a work of the 15th century that contains treasures such as: the Choir-Stall and the Chapel of St. James by Antonio da San Gallo the Younger. Nearby, in the Church of Saint Luigi dei Francesi, some of the fundamental masterpieces of Italian art can be admired: the three large canvasses by Caravaggio, highest examples of paint-ing after Michelangelo, dating from the end of the 16th century: the Calling of St. Matthew, the Martyrdom of Matthew and St. Mathew and the Angel.

Caravaggio's paintings stand out for their innova-tive and disturbing realism, and for the unusual use of light, even in his own day, so much so that the last of these three paintings was deemed unfit for a church because St. Matthew ap-pears as a tired old man with dirty feet.

Via Veneto and Via Condotti

The two names synonymous of elegance and high society throughout the world are via Condotti and via Veneto.

Via Condotti is at the centre of a network of streets (via Borgognona, via Mario dei Fiori, via Bocca di Leone) and is crowded with elegant boutiques, such as Ferragamo, Hermes, Gucci, Valentino, Versace and it is a pleasure to take a walk there especially late in the afternoon. It is usual to stop at the Caffe Greco, which is the oldest and most famous in Rome.

It was founded by a Greek in 1760 and became in the 19th cent-ury a meeting place for such illustrious men as Goethe, Stendhal, Byron, Wagner and Berlioz. This same atmosphere still survives especially in the delightful little rooms at the back.

The long and winding street that goes from the Porta Pinciana is via Vittorio Veneto, better known throughout the world as "via Veneto". Many embassies (includ-ing the American one) line the avenue as do expensive hotels and well-known cafés (such as the Café de Paris). In the sixties this avenue was, thanks to the film La Dolce Vita by Fellini, a favourite of Romans and the jet-set.

Today it has lost some of its charms, but it is pleasant to take a walk here, perhaps stopping in an out-of-the-way spot where there is a very different atmosphere: the Church of Santa Maria della Concezione, built by the Capucin friars. The crypt contains hundreds of skeletons.

The Obelisks
symbols of the sun and immortality

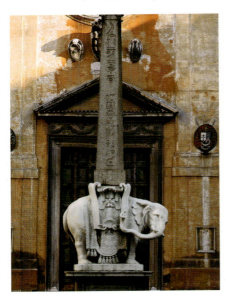

Rome, more than any other city, is full of obelisks, many of Egyptian origin. These enormous monoliths, either bare or covered in hieroglyphics, form focus points at the centre of the great squares; but they are also symbols of the sun and immortality. There are thirteen obelisks in Rome. The most ancient and the highest (31 metres of red granite) is perhaps the Obelisk in Piazza S.Giovanni in Laterano that goes back to the 15th century BC. It was brought to Rome in 357 AD and erected here in 1587 by Pope Sixtus V, who had a fondness for these monuments. To him we owe the erection of the most celebrated Roman obelisk, that of St. Peter's Square. The Vatican's monolith made of red granite is 25,31 metres high and devoid of hieroglyphics. It was brought to Rome by Caligula and in 1586 Pope Sixtus V had it placed in front of the Basilica. It is said that the transporting was very difficult and required hundreds of horses and men. A year later, the same Sixtus V had another obelisk placed on the Esquiline hill, it is a bare 14,75 metres high and without hieroglyphics. The fourth Obelisk of Sixtus V is splendid and placed in the famous Piazza del Popolo. It is almost 24 metres high and has hieroglyphics from 1200 BC; it was brought to Rome at the time of Augustus in celebration of the victory over Egypt. It was then Bernini's turn to erect another two obelisks: the one in Piazza Navona (almost 17 metres high and rich in hieroglyphics) and that in Piazza Minerva, almost 5,47 metres high and supported by a small elephant (designed by Bernini). In front of the Pantheon is another obelisk, called Macuteo, only six metres high and dating from the time of Ramses II. Dating from the end of the 18th century is the Obelisk of the Quirinale (placed in 1786 it is 16,63 metres high and made of red granite) and from the same epoch the Obelisk on the Trinità dei Monti. ❯❯

The Pantheon of all Saints
the best-preserved and mysterious of ancient monuments

Built a few years before the birth of Christ by Marcus Agrippa in honour of Augustus, it was then restructured under Hadrian (around 120 AD), the Pantheon is the most imposing and complete building surviving from an-tiquity. It is so well preserved because from 608 AD it was converted into a church dedicated to the Madonna and therefore cherished by the pontiffs. It is complex because it mixes varying geometrical shapes (square, sphere, cylinder) and because it fuses two architectural styles: that typical of the temples (the pronaos) and the round plan characteristic of the thermal baths. A cylindrical wall, six metres thick, supports the dome. The dome is 43,30 metres high and wide. It is the biggest vault ever made of masonry and is bigger even than St. Peter's. In the centre of the dome is an opening nine meters wide, the only source of light. Inside there is a great central niche of mauve marble, and six smaller niches around it inlayed in multicoloured marble; the interplay of their colours fill the temple with a haunting light. Many artists are buried here: Perin del Vaga, Annibale Carracci, Taddeo Zuccari and Raphael. The Pantheon also contains tombs of members of the Savoy family, King Vittorio Emanuele II and King Umberto I. ❯❯

120

« The bridges over the Tiber and Castel Sant'Angelo
crossing the river

Many bridges cross the Tiber, some of them dating from the time of ancient Rome. The smallest is the footbridge Fabricius (62 BC), the oldest Roman bridge to have survived, still used as a link between the Tiberina island and the city, as does the Cestius bridge, restored by the Byzantines in 370 AD. The ruins of the of the Ponte Emilio, of which only one arcade is still standing, are very picturesque. It was the first bridge built in stone

in the 2nd century BC and is today known as the Ponte Rotto (Broken Bridge). The Ponte Milvio, to the North of Rome, is famous because here Constantine fought and won a battle against Maxentius in 312 AD. There are also more recent bridges: Ponte Sisto built in 1473 and enlarged in the 19th century; today it is closed to traffic. The splendid Ponte Sant' Angelo links Castel Sant'Angelo to Campo Marzio. This bridge was built in the 2nd century AD and since 1530 has been adorned by statues of St. Paul (by Paolo Taccone) and St. Peter (by Lorenzetto). In mid-17th century Pope Clement IX had the statues of ten angels, designed by Bernini and sculpted by his pupils, placed on the balustrade. Castel Sant'Angelo was built by the Emperor Hadrian as a mausoleum for himself. It was finished in 130 AD. Initially a statue of the Emperor was placed on the terrace of the castle, now replaced by a sculpture of an angel. The entrance to the Castle is through the Courtyard Salvatore that leads into the Courtyard of the Angel where cannon balls are stocked. Michelangelo designed the double line of windows on the back wall. The many rooms in the Castle are extremely interesting; on the third floor is the courtyard of Alexander VI which is embellished by a charming well. It is followed by the bathroom of Clement VII decorated by Giovanni da Udine. Not to be missed are the historical prisons, called the Mouth of Hell, where such people as Cellini, Giordano Bruno and Cagliostro were imprisoned. Finally, there is the Treasury and the beautiful Library. »

Tiberina Island

Campo dei Fiori is a very popular meeting place in Rome. It is located between via Vittorio Emanuele and the Tiber. The Campo dei Fiori was

Campo dei fiori

not always a happy place as the statue of Giordano Bruno reminds us, for here it was that criminals were publicly executed and where the philosopher Giordano Bruno was burnt at the stake. However, today things have considerably changed; there is a lively market held every day. There are many other things to see in the vicinity: the old Jewish Ghetto, the Tiberina Island in the shape of a boat and dedicated by the Romans to Esculapius the god of medicine. Today, there is a Hospital called San Giovanni di Dio on the island. There are three bridges that link the island to the city, two of which are the Ponte Fabricius (still intact) and the Ponte Rotto (an arch of the16th century is all that remains); and not far from here are the Palazzo Farnese and the Palazzo Spada.

Churches and Basilicas

San Giovanni in Laterano

The Basilica of San Giovanni in Laterano is perhaps the most ancient of Christian churches. It is held to be the most important after Saint Peter's, because it is the Cathedral of Rome. In the central space between the transepts is an altar where only the Pope, the bishop of Rome, can celebrate mass. As in all major basilicas, the entrance is preceded by a large portico; here is placed a statue of Constantine. The basilica has five doors; the one on the extreme right can only be opened during Holy Year, like Saint Peter's.

The façade of San Giovanni in Laterano is a masterpiece by Alessandro Galilei (1732-1735) showing strong influences of the Baroque and neo-classical. Fifteen colossal statues crown the façade, the most conspicuous being that of Christ.

The evocative and beautiful interior has five naves built in 1650 by Francesco Borromini. The transept is earlier and contains a beautiful tabernacle by Giovanni di Stefano.

The left side of the transept leads to the extraordinary Cloister, a true masterpiece of the 13th century by the Vassalletto family. Very close to the church is an antique Baptistery commissioned by Constantine at the same time as the basilica; it is octagonal and in the centre is a green basalt urn, once a baptismal font.

Interior of the Basilica

Santa Maria Maggiore

This grandiose church stands on the Esquiline Hill. It was built under the pontificate of Sixtus III in the early 15th cent-ury and its Romanesque bell tower is the highest in Rome (75 metres).

The mid-18th century façade has five arches and a loggia by Ferdinando Fuga (in the loggia lovely mosaics from a previous façade). Inside there are three naves, a beautiful pavement with geometric designs, and a coffered ceiling by Giuliano da Sangallo. Along the central nave are thirty six mosaic panels depicting scenes from the Old Testament.

The mosaics over the Triumphal Arch, which represent scenes from the Life of Jesus and the Virgin and those over the apse by Iacopo Torriti (1295), are beautiful. These mosaics, which span several centuries, are amongst the most precious and beautiful in existence.

Noteworthy are also the chapels of this basilica: the Sistine Chapel (built by Domenico Fontana for Pope Sixtus V) and the Paolina Chapel (built by Flaminio Ponzi for Pope Paul V).

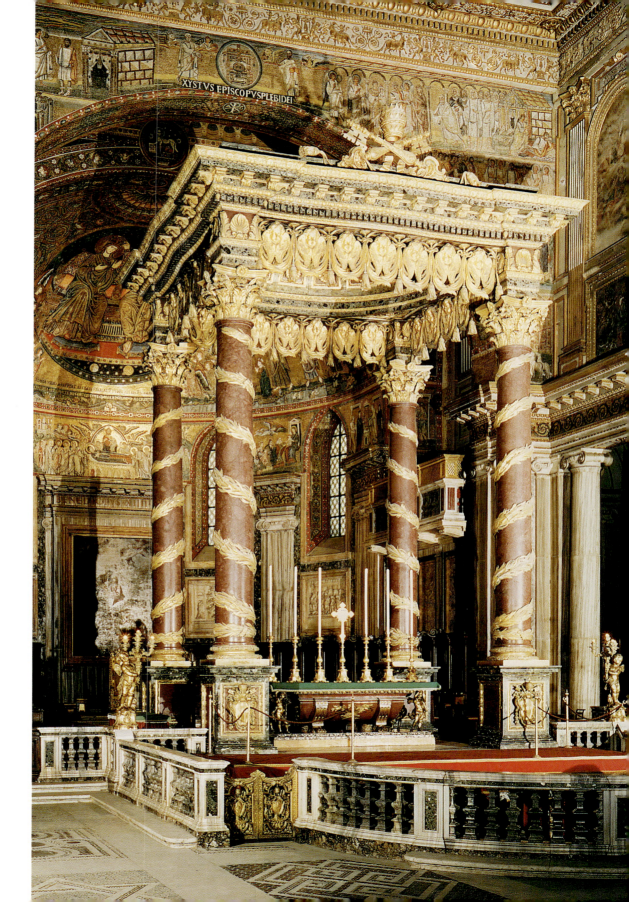

San Paolo fuori le Mura

One hundred and thirty metres long and 65 meters wide, this is the second largest basilica in Rome after St. Peter's. Started under the reign of Constantine, it was completed in 395 AD. Over the centuries it was enriched with paintings and frescoes until in July 823 AD a terrible fire almost burnt it to the ground.

The basilica was rebuilt in 1928 following the original design (including the portico in front of the façade, called "the hundred columns"). Inside there are many works of art: the Byzantine-Venetian mosaics in the apse, the Gothic Ciborium by Arnolfo di Cambio, in the Chapel of the Holy Sacrament the mosaic representing the Holy Virgin, the frieze with mosaic portraits of the Popes, the Triumphal Arch at the far end of the central nave, the Byzantine bronze panels of the Holy Door, and the harmonious cloister with multicoloured marbles, mosaics and smooth and spiral-shaped columns.

San Pietro in Vincoli

This very old church, dedicated to the Apostles, was erected in the 4th century and completely renovated by Pope Julius II at the end of the 15th century.

It owes its name to the relic it contains ("in vincoli", "enchained"), namely the chains that bound St. Peter in Jerusalem and later in Rome (they are kept in a gilded bronze urn). The other great attraction of the church is the Mausoleum of Julius II, an unfinished work by Michelangelo.

He worked on it from 1513 to 1516 and it was originally destined to stand in St. Peter's. For the mausoleum he sculpted the famous Statue of Moses and the two Prisoners, now in the Louvre.

Michelangelo, Moses

St. Clement

Few basilicas are of so many different styles and have been added to as frequently, as the Basilica of St. Clement. The original early-Christian basilica was built on a pre-existing Roman building of the time of Domitian (the remains can be visited) dating from the end of the 4th century and dedicated to the third Pope, Clement. At the beginning of the 13th century, the actual basilica was built over the old one, which was discovered during excavations at the end of the last century. The façade of the Basilica is preceded by an atrium and a pronaos, whilst in the middle of the central nave is a Schola Cantorum. The mosaic that covers the apse is magnificent and represents the Triumph of the Cross. Very lovely are the 15th century frescoes by Masolino di Panicale in the Chapel of St. Catherine.

The early Medieval frescoes are extremely interesting and form a complete cycle dedicated to St. Clement and others illustrating the Legend of Sisinius that can be visited in the lower basilica.

Santa Maria in Trastevere

The first church to be dedicated to the Madonna, and amongst the oldest in Rome, has undergone many changes: from the foundation dating from around 340 AD until the recent restorations of the

19th century – not very good. The church has three naves and assumed its present aspect under Pope Innocent II who had the sanctuary reconstructed in the 12th century, ornamenting the apse with splendid mosaics, under Byzantine influence. These mosaics represent on the triumphal arch the Prophets, Symbols of the Evangelists, the Apocalypse, and the Cross. In the semi-circular recess of the apse is the extremely beautiful mosaic of Christ crowning the Virgin; beneath the mosaics, the cycle of the life of Mary by Pietro Cavallini (end of the 12th century). The church stands in the popular district of Trastevere.

Santa Maria in Aracoeli

The church was begun in the 14th century by the Franciscans, while the marble staircase – a votive offering for a deliverance from the plague – was added in the middle of the same century. Inside there are three naves. Noteworthy the lovely pavement, by the Cosmati and the richly decorated wooden coffered ceiling (in the middle the Virgin with Child). Here are one of the most loved and venerated images of the Romans (in the left transept): the statue of the Holy Child which is said to have been sculpted from an olive tree from Gethsemane and which is held to be miraculous. Noteworthy are the Stories of San Bernardino, a 15th century masterpiece by Pinturicchio. Over the main altar is the panel depicting a Madonna with Child (a work dating from around 1000 AD), to whom is dedicated the grandiose staircase in front of the church.

Santa Maria in Cosmedin

Built in the 4th century, this church was also constructed on an ancient Roman building and takes its name from the Greek word meaning "embellished".
Beneath the portico in front of the façade, is the Mouth of Truth, an ancient lid in the shape of a mask. According to legend any liar who puts his hand into the slit will have his it snapped off.
Although the church has no masterpieces, it is rich in interesting objects: the elegant
Romanesque bell tower, the richlydecorated pavements and the Gothic canopy protecting the main altar. Visit the Crypt dug in tuff, perhaps the remains of an antique pagan altar.

Sant'Andrea della Valle

This church is noteworthy for its beautiful dome (a 17th century work by Maderno on an octagonal drum) the highest in Rome after St. Peter's. The church was built at the end of the 16th century by Pietro Paolo Olivieri and the aforementioned Maderno. The façade, however, is from the mid-17th century, and was built by Rainaldi and Fontana. The fresco decorating the vault of the dome represents the Glory of Paradise by Lanfranco, and in the curve of the apse are three frescoes by Mattia Preti (1540) telling the story of the Martyrdom of St. Andrew. From St. Peter's come the two tombs of Popes Pius II and III, both members of the Piccolomini family.

The Museums

Rome is, above all, a city of museums and the artistic wealth collected here is quite unique.
The main museums of the capital contain, as we shall see, mainly classical antiquities; because of their size and quality this collection has no equal.

Capitolini Museums

These museums display the oldest collection of Roman antiquities and are located in the Piazza del Campidoglio; they were founded in 1471 by Sixtus IV. The Museo del Palazzo dei Conservatori is one of the museums and displays Greek and Roman sculptures. One of the most striking is Apollo shooting an arrow and an Athena, both from the 5th century BC. Quite extraordinary is the Venus from the Esquiline of a much later date (1st century BC). The Head of Costantine, a huge bronze, is the first of sixty five busts of Roman Emperors in the collection; amongst these are Augustus, Nero, Trajan, Marcus Aurelius and Caracalla. In the Sala dei Conservatori is the admirable and famous Capitoline Wolf, symbol of Rome, bronze work of the 5th century BC attributed to the followers of Vulca from Veio (who decorated the Capitoline Jupiter).

The Dying Gladiator

Caravaggio, the young St. John

The twins under the she-wolf are, as is well known, a 15th century addition by Antonio del Pollaiolo. In the Capitoline Museum is what is generally considered to be one of the most beautiful sculptures of antiquity: the Dying Gladiator, a marble copy of a bronze from Pergamum of the 3rd century BC representing a dying warrior. It was found in the Sallustian Gardens in the 16th century. Among other masterpieces is the Capitoline Venus, a Roman copy of an original Hellenistic work.
In the Pinacoteca Capitolina is a collection of paintings from the 16th and 17th centuries: Titian, Lotto, Rubens (Romulus and Remus suckling the she-wolf), the splendid Portrait of a Man by Velazquez, the Young St. John the Baptist and the Fortune Teller, both by Caravaggio.

Colossal statue of Constantine

Ippolito Caffi, the Papal Blessing from St. Peter's

Museo Nazionale Romano

This museum, in an ex-convent near the Baths of Diocletian, displays a large quantity of Roman works, the most striking coming from excavations in and around Rome.

Perhaps the most outstanding work is the celebrated Ludovisi Throne of the 5th century BC. Archaeologists and art historians have discussed at great length its authenticity.

The Tiber Apollo is also exceptional; it is a copy of an original Greek work possibly by Phidias. The Reclining Warrior is, however, an original bronze from the Hellenistic period: a splendid sculpture of great strength. The Niobe from the Gardens of Sallust is very beautiful and is one of the first examples of a female nude, a copy of a Greek work of the 5th century BC. The most moving and compelling masterpiece is probably the Hellenistic statue called the Young Girl of Anzio; it was discovered in a niche at Anzio in the last century.

Museo Nazionale di Villa Giulia

This museum is placed in a splendid 16th century villa that was built by Vignola for Julius II. It was founded at the end of the 19th century and contains an archaeological collection of pre-Roman works. The Sarcophagus of the Married Couple is an Etruscan sculpture in baked clay from the 6th century BC in which the two figures express noble serenity and elegance. The Apollo and Herakles is a splendid and majestic life-size sculpture; the admirable Cistae Ficoroni is from the 4th century BC.

This museum, one of the most modern and well-stocked, displays the reconstruction of a tomb from the necropolis of Cerveteri.

The Sarcophagus of the married couple

Other museums

A complete visit of the museums in Rome would take weeks. It is important to see the Museum of Castel Sant'Angelo (to see the prisons but also the Sala Paolina and the ancient weapons). You should also visit the San Luca Academy Gallery (there are works of art by Raphael, Guercino and Rubens). The Museum of Modern Art, where is a collection of Italian paintings and sculptures of the 19th and 20th centuries, also deserves a visit.

Palaces and Galleries

Galleria Borghese

The Casino Borghese stands in the beautiful park of the Villa Borghese . The country-house was planned by Ponzio in 1608 and a few years later finished by Giovanni Vasanzio. At the wish of Cardinal Scipione, nephew of Pope Paul V, the surroundings were landscaped; the building now houses the Museum, which contains the superb collection that belonged to the aforesaid cardinal.

The most famous work is the Statue of Paolina Bonaparte, Napoleon's sister, as Venus, admirably sculptured in the neoclassical style by Canova (1805). Sensuality has been imprisoned in the smoothest of polished marbles; Paolina posed in the nude, defying the prejudices of her age. The David by Bernini (1624) is a masterpiece. David as been captured in a tense pose – very different from the statue of the same name by Michelangelo. The Apollo and Daphne by Bernini tells the fable from Ovid in which Daphne fleeing from Apollo is transformed into a tree. Another masterpiece by Bernini is the Rape of Proserpine. The main motif lies in the differing tensions of the two bodies: Pluto is a muscular gladiator, while Proserpine is in a simple and delicate pose.

The most outstanding paintings in the Galleria Borghese are: Sacred and Profane Love, early work of Titian (1514). The artist's finesse is revealed rather by the splendour of the colours than by the symbolic message

Raphael, Deposition

Caravaggio, Madonna dei Palafrenieri

Bernini, Rape of Proserpine

Canova, Paolina Borghese

of the two female figures: one nude, the other dressed. The Danae by Correggio (1530) is an extremely sensual work of art; the Deposition by Raphael was inspired by an ancient sarcophagus. Finally there are the magnificent paintings by Caravaggio; Saint Jerome (1606), an excellent portrait (the horizontal layout is unusual), and the Madonna dei Palafrenieri painted by Caravaggio in 1605 for the church of the same name: it was refused because of its realism and found its way to the Borghese collection. Under St. Anne's gaze the Madonna, a ravishing peasant, and the Child, boldly nude, trample the snake representing the Evil One.

Doria Pamphilj Gallery

In the Rococo style palace of the same name, many times restructured (the façade on the Corso and that on via del Plebiscito are of the mid-18th century), is the splendid Gallery (still

Caravaggio, Rest on the flight into Egypt

owned by the Doria Pamphilj) containing a wealth of masterpieces (including the sumptuous Appartamenti di Rappresentanza which can be visited). Titian's Salomé, an early work, and the Madonna with Child by Parmigianino. In Caravaggio's youthful work, Rest on the Flight into Egypt, the artist is still far from the tragic mood of his maturity. The paintings of Carracci, Savoldo and Salvator Rosa are important. Among the many works by non-Italians is a superb portrait of Innocent X by Velazquez (1650), some landscapes amongst which Landscape with Dancers by Claude Lorrain, a genuine masterpiece because of the admirable contrast between the clear sky and the dark wood. Noteworthy are also two Busts of Innocent X by Bernini. The entrance to the Gallery is from Piazza del Collegio Romano.

Spada Gallery

This Gallery is in the 16th century Palazzo Spada, which is worth visiting in itself. Today it is the seat of the State Council. The palace was restructured in the 17th century by the Spada family. The stucco statues of ancient Roman noblemen have been replaced recently in the niches of the façade. The perspective gallery by Borromini is superb (difficult to imagine that it is actually only nine metres long). The Gallery exhibits many important works of art especially from the 17th century: Guido Reni, Guercino and Valentin.
Finally in the Salone delle Adunanze is the colossal statue presumed to be of Pompey.

Barberini Palace

Another Roman palace worth visiting for its splendour, and the collection it houses (Galleria Nazionale di Arte Antica). The palace belonged to the Barberini Family, who owned nearly all

Caravaggio, Judith and Holofernes

the district, and is attributed to Carlo Maderno. Later the two great artists, Bernini and Borromini, worked on it. Bernini designed the façade overlooking the garden and the staircase; Borromini the spiral staircase and the windows of the top storey. The frescoed ceilings of many rooms are extremely lovely, especially the vast Triumph of Divine Providence by Pietro da Cortona. Inside the Barberini Palace (since 1949 property of the Italian State) is the famous Galleria d'Arte Antica, containing works by Filippo Lippi, Lorenzo Lotto, Andrea Del Sarto, Perugino and Caravaggio. Among the non-Italian painters are Holbein and Nicolas Poussin. Probably the greatest masterpiece in the gallery is the Portrait of the Fornarina by Raphael in which he uses his plebeian mistress as a model (some attribute this work to Giulio Romano). Do not miss the Portrait of Stefano IV Colonna by Bronzino. There is an admirable painting by Caravaggio Judith and Holofernes, which he painted this work during his stay in Rome under the patronage of Cardinal del Monte. The strong contrast between light and shade and its tragic realism are typical of the artist's style and provoked great controversy.

Farnese Palace

It is the biggest private palace in Rome. It was built for Cardinal Farnese (who later became Pope Paul III) first by Antonio da Sangallo the younger and then by Michelangelo, who finished the upper storeys, added the entablature and part of the courtyard. The façade and the loggia giving onto via Giulia were finished by Giacomo Della Porta. Today the palace houses the French Embassy. Some of the most beautiful parts of this building are: the façade, which is built, so it is said, using materials from ancient Rome; the extremely elegant courtyard with its rows of columns, windows and arcades.
Inside the palace are the Sala dei Fasti (with frescoes by Zuccari) and the Sala delle Guardie (with a copy of the Farnese Hercules, the original is in Naples).
The Gallery was frescoed in the early 16th century by the brothers Annibale and Agostino Carraci.

Palazzo Venezia

The Palazzo Venezia was built in the mid-15th century and is the first example of a Roman Renaissance palace although, because of its bulk and its crenelations, it brings to mind a Medieval building. Its attribution to Leon Battista Alberti is not certain. The history of the palace is a long one: it was first the Venetian Embassy, then it became the Austrian Embassy, and was returned to Italy in 1916. From the balcony on the first floor Benito Mussolini, Fascist dictator who had his office here from 1929 to 1943, made some of his most famous speeches. The Museum of the same name today holds collections of tapestries, sculptures, church silver, arms and pottery. Visit the Sala del Mappa Mondo where Mussolini's office was.

The great roman libraries
three million years of words

A third of the manuscripts preserved in the world are found in Italy and a great number of them are kept in the Roman libraries where there is a collection of millions of books both antique and rare. Among the great Roman libraries the most outstanding is the Vaticana, one of the most prestigious in the world. It was founded in 1475 in order to contain the papal archives where they are still kept today. Sixtus V had this building constructed by Domenico Fontana. It contains two million books and a

further hundred and fifty thousand manuscripts housed in the basements. The main library in Rome is the National Library Vittorio Emanuele II (viale Castro Pretorio). It was inaugurated in 1876 and then moved to the present building in 1975; it holds five million printed documents, six thousand periodicals and five thousand manuscripts. You can also consult over sixty thousand microfilms that give you a list of what is preserved in a hundred Italian libraries. The Casanatense Library was founded by the Dominicans and during the 18th century was the leading library in Rome. It has almost four hundred thousand printed documents and six thousand five hundred manuscripts and specialises in religious culture and the 18th century. The Angelica Library was the first library opened to the public in Rome (1614); today it contains, in a splendid building two hundred thousand works and two thousand five hundred manuscripts (the first edition, 1472, of the Divine Comedy by Foligno and the De Oratore, the first book to be printed in Italy in 1465). The Valiccelliana Library is another important Roman library and founded by Saint Filippo Neri (mainly works on history and theology); the Lincei Library founded in 1754 has a large section on Islam and the Biblioteca Universitaria Alessandrina (1661) holds more than one million volumes on philosophy, history, literature and law. 》

Rome under Fascism
the illusions and reality of the regime

Fascism left its mark on Rome, especially in certain districts and buildings: the district of the EUR, the Foro Italico and the construction, only possible because of vast urban demolitions, of what was called the via dell'Impero and via della Conciliazione. Mussolini wanted to revive the great glories of ancient Rome and therefore intended to build an enormous Palazzo del Fascio next to the old Forum, but this was never carried out. Under Fascism, however, the EUR complex was built (it was to have held the Universal Exhibition of Rome in 1942, but because of the war it never took place), an architecture meant

to demonstrate the triumphs of the regime but which, paradoxically, proved to be an excellent example of rational of architecture In the EUR district stands the Palazzo della Civiltà e del Lavoro (1938-1943) on five floors with false arches that wanted to imitate the Coliseum and reminds us of certain metaphysical paintings of De Chirico. The Foro Italico at the foot of Monte Mario is a large sporting complex where stands the Stadio dei Marmi (1932: twenty thousand spectators, sixty statues of athletes) and the gigantic Obelisk weighing three hundred tons and eighteen metres high. Near the Foro Italico is the great Olympic Stadium of Rome, built in 1953; it seats eighty thousand people. Mussolini planned to build a large boulevard – which he would have called via dell'Impero – linking Piazza Venezia to the Coliseum. Nine hundred metres long and thirty metres wide, this street was built over mounds of ruins and rubble (taken partly during the levelling of the Velia Hill, one of the seven Roman hills) and the Roman Forum was thus artificially divided from the Imperial Forums. This Fascist imprint caused irreparable damage to the historical centre and the archaeological excavations of ancient Rome. Via della Conciliazione, a large boulevard going towards St. Peter's Square, was built, amidst serious controversy, between 1936 and 1950. In order to build it Piacentini, the architect, demolished old districts and pulled down churches and palaces. 》

The Appian Way

This is the most famous, the longest, the straightest of the old Roman roads and also the best preserved. It starts, more or less, from the Baths of Caracalla and in an almost straight line, a good ninety kilometres, joins Terracina, Capua (in Campania), then goes through Benevento until it gets to Brindisi.

It was the outlet of ancient Rome for traffic going East. It was called the "regina viarum", "queen of the roads". Begun in 312 BC by Appius Claudius, a censor who gave it his name, it was extended to Brindisi around 190 BC. It fell into disuse at the end of the Empire, was "rediscovered" during the Renaissance but was only restored in our century. It was built using extremely high standards of engineering (it is only in this century that this technology was rediscovered). The Appian Way consists of four different and paved strata four metres and ten centimetres wide, sidewalks on either side, and at the time of the ancient Romans was lined with trees. Many patrician tombs line it as it was customary then to bury the dead outside the city walls.

To whoever travels along it today the Appian Way gives rise to powerful pictures – of wagons, people, armies, travelling merchants – and because of the many ancient tombs, the sacredness of death.

The tomb of Cecilia Metella is certainly the most famous. This young patrician girl's tomb is in the style of an Etruscan tumulus and anticipates the great mausoleums of Augustus and Hadrian. On a square stone base rises a cylindrical construction that encloses the small funeral chamber. The tomb, today decorated by Medieval crenelations, was surmounted by a pensile grove of cypresses.

There are many important monuments along the Appian Way and in its surroundings. The enormous, well-preserved Baths of Caracalla, today used for summer operatic performances, could accommodate some one thousand six hundred bathers and were built towards 212 AD by the Emperor Caracalla.

It has gymnasiums, baths, music rooms and underground rooms. Except for a few traces of the old mosaic pavement, all the decorations have disappeared. Two famous ancient works were excavated here: the Farnese Hercules and the Farnese Taurus.

The Catacombs

Catacombs of Priscilla, central Gallery to the first floor

Etimologically the word "catacomba" derives from Latin "ad catacumbas" (near the cavity).

The catacombs are underground burial-places, dug by the first Christians between the 2nd and the 3rd century to bury their deads and among them some martyrs, too; their presence made the Catacombs real veneration places and this import has remained unaltered during the centuries till now.

For a long time it has been believed that these underground places were the ones where the first Christians hid to flee from persecutions. It has been on the contrary proved by now they were not secret places at all but well-known burial areas which were guarded by the Roman authorities of the time. Only the scarcity of free spaces seems to be the reason why these first christian cemeteries were underground.

As well as other burial-places they were situated outside the city walls and along consular roads constituting another city, an underground ring which extends for hundreds of kilometres of galleries.

The subsoil, being above all formed by tuff, has caused the development of such a burial method. The most famous catacombs are those of San Sebastiano, Domitilla and San Callisto.

In the Catacombs of San Sebastiano, along the Appian Way, besides the crypt of San Sebastian several inscriptions and decorations with animals

Catacombs of San Sebastiano, view of the three sepulchres

Catacombs of San Callisto, Crypt of the popes

(symbols for the Christians of the time) can be admired.

The Catacombs of Domitilla are situated on Via delle Sette Chiese 282 near the above-mentioned old appian way. The place where they have been dug seems to have been donated by the roman matron they have been dedicated to.

Of particular interest are the Basilica of the Santi Martiri Nereo and Achilleo of the 4th century, the hypogeum of the Flavi and several frescoes with scenes from the New and Old Testament.

In the catacombs of San Callisto, situated on the old Appian Way, are the crypt of the Papi Martiri, dated back to the 3rd century, on which the homonymous saint, saint Urban and the face of Christ are represented.

The statue of Saint Cecily by Carlo Maderno and the cubicles of the Sacraments are particular interest.

 rome

Surroundings

Far from the noise of the city, in the peace of the surrounding countryside, among the pine trees, heralds of the sea Rome has many superb walks, the first one being in old Ostia.

Old Ostia

Of the antique Roman port, built in the 6th century BC, there still remain houses, taverns, patrician villas, temples and fountains which stand amidst lush vegetation. The most notable excavations are the Mithraeum, the Egyptian temples and the synagogue. Not to be missed is the Museo Ostiense. In the beautiful Theatre of Augustus famous classical performances are held during the summer. You can go down the Tiber by boat from here to Rome: a picturesque and nostalgic journey.

rome

Tivoli

Tivoli is situated on the banks of the river Aniene near the famous falls where Roman patricians used to build their summer residences. Here is the famous Hadrian Villa, the largest and richest ancient Roman villa built after 100 AD. The complex contains the Academy, the Poikile (a rectangular peristyle with a central fish-pond), the Canopus (a long narrow basin built in a natural hollow). The Villa d'Este and the Villa Gregoriana date from the Renaissance period.
The former, built by Pirro Ligorio in 1550 for Cardinal Ippolito II of Este, stands in the famous park decorated by delightful fountains and small cascades.
Near the Villa Gregoriana are the famous Cascades of the river Aniene which flow down picturesquely amid a rocky landscape.
This spot inspired the great writer Marguerite Yourcenar to write her famous novel Hadrian's Memoirs.

Roman Castles

A visit to the picturesque towns known as Castelli Romani (Roman Castles) makes
a delightful Sunday outing. Located south of Rome they are renowned for their excellent food
and wine.

In Frascati, of great interest is Villa Aldobrandini, whose immense façade gives onto a
luxuriant park. Villa Falconieri is also very beautiful but can be visited only on request. Worth
a visit is also the interesting Abbazia di Grottaferrata, an abbey built around 1000 AD. Not to
be missed is Castel Gandolfo, the Pope's summer residence. Our visit ends with the town of
Palestrina, famous for the ruins of the old city walls and for the huge Sanctuary of Fortune.

rome

The Vatican City

We now visit the Vatican City before we move on to important masterpieces and sacred memorials. It is the smallest state in the world (0,44 kilometres) and is located on the hill of the same name, between the hills Monte Mario and Monte Gianicolo.

Here, where the Emperor Caligula had built a circus and Saint Peter was martyred in 67 AD, rises the most important basilica in the Christian world.

The Vatican State was established during the Middle Ages and it grew to include most of central Italy. Wiped out by the Unification of Italy in 1870, the state was re-established in 1929 and ratified by the Lateran Treaty between the Holy See and the Italian State. The Vatican State has its own police, diplomatic corps and army, including the famous Swiss Guards. They were founded in 1506 by Julius II. Originally two hundred Swiss guards made up the Pope's personal guard. Their evocative uniforms, the design attributed to Michelangelo, have remained unchanged for five centuries.

Piazza San Pietro

Saint Peter's Square, the centre of Christianity for over a thousand years, is artistically and religiously moving.

It is a huge place, harmoniously open to the heavens, a perfect ellipse two hundred and forty metres wide, and surrounded by magnificent colonnades by Bernini. It contains two hundred and eighty-four Doric pillars set in four rows and surmounted on the entablature by one hundred and forty statues of Saints and Martyrs.

There are two great fountains on each side by Maderno and at the centre, in 1586, an Egyptian Obelisk was placed (a relic of the True Cross is kept on its summit).

There are two interesting things to look out for in this square: by standing between the two fountains, on a round porphyry slab, the two hundred and eighty four pillars seem set perfectly in a row and only the first column is visible; to the right of the basilica are the apostolic palaces, between which the Sistine Chapel is visible.

On its triangular shaped roof can be seen the famous chimney from which comes the white smoke announcing that a new Pope has been elected.

Saint Peter's Basilica

Here at one time was Nero's Circus, here St. Peter was martyred and the Apostles were buried. Because of this, Constantine, newly converted to Christianity, had built on this very spot a basilica around which Pope Symmachus in 500 AD built the first residence of the bishop of Rome. Throughout the centuries the district grew in size. Here it was on Christmas Day (800 AD) that on the tomb of St. Peter, and not in the cathedral of Rome (which was then the church of S. Giovanni in Laterano), that Leo III crowned Charlemagne. In 1377 the exiled Popes returning from Avignon, established the Curia here until Julius II decided to build in the place of the old basilica of Constantine, now become unsafe, a new splendid church; the work was entrusted to the architect Bramante. The building of this church took more than a hundred and fifty years. On the death of Bramante in 1514, Raphael took over, followed by Antonio da Sangallo the Younger, who continued until 1546 when the task was finally passed on to Michelangelo, who decided on a church in the shape of a Greek cross and designed the dome, but he only saw it completed as far as the drum.

Later, Paul V entrusted Carlo Maderno to revert to the Latin cross, to add three chapels on each side, and to build the façade; the latter was built between 1606 and 1614 but was criticised because too large in proportion to its height. In 1646 Bernini, certainly the greatest Baroque architect, was entrusted to reconstruct the façade; he had the superb idea of building an immense elliptical colonnade for the square. The crowning feature of St. Peter's is the grandiose dome by

Swiss Guards

Michelangelo visible from every part of the city. The dome stands on a drum which has a series of windows surmounted by elegant pediments, alternately semi-circular and triangular, separated by double columns. You get to the dome by climbing five hundred and thirty seven steps or by using the elevator: from the top you can enjoy a lovely view of Rome. The sphere that crowns the dome's lantern is so big it can hold a few people. In front of the façade is a portico by Maderno containing the equestrian statues of Constantine (by Bernini), the first Christian Emperor and Charlemagne (by Cornacchini), the first Emperor of the Holy Roman Empire. Five doors lead into the basilica. The last door on the right is the Holy Door, only opened during the Holy Year, the middle door is the 4th century so-called Door of Filarete and the last door on the left is the recent Door of Death (1964) done by Giacomo Manzù for Pope John XXIII.

nside the Basilica

Here we are in the sublime, harmonious vastness of the biggest Christian church. It is over two hundred and ten metres long and the dome is a hundred and thirty six metres high. A good idea of the vastness of it all is obtained by bearing in mind that the putti (baby angels) are bigger than a man, while the immense central canopy is as high as a Roman palace.

There are so many things to see, that we can but discuss the most important: the Pietà by Michelangelo, sculptured by the great artist (who was not yet twenty five years old), for the jubilee of 1500 AD. It is the only work signed by the artist (his name is carved on the sash of the Madonna). This work of extraordinary beauty is totally different from the tragic Pietàs sculptured later by Michelangelo; in this one, for example, the Madonna is depicted, strangely enough, like a girl.

Michelangelo, Pietà.

Also important are: the bronze Baldachin by Bernini and the beautiful and venerated statue of St. Peter.

The Baldachin is a gigantic baroque structure upheld by spiral pillars, cast using the bronze decorations from the Pantheon. It was placed over the papal high altar which is actually over the Tomb of St. Peter (1624-1633). The eighty nine lights of the hemycycle are kept permanently lit to illuminate the tomb of St. Peter.

Years later Alexander VII entrusted Bernini to redesign the apse. The artist conceived a reliquary throne in gilded bronze, large Baroque construction protecting the wooden throne, considered to be the true throne of St. Peter. Surmounted by a bright glory of rays and by the dove of the Holy Spirit, it is crowded by innumerable figures in gilded stucco. There are two great sepulchral monuments on each side: the tomb of Pope Paul III (1575, by Guglielmo Della Porta) and the Tomb of Pope Urban VIII (1647, by Bernini). By the dome's pillars are four Statues of Saints, amongst which St. Longinus by Bernini (in his hand is the spear that pierces the body of Christ).

We conclude our visit with the Sacristy and the Museum of Saint Peter's Treasury, where we find a precious Ciborium by Donatello and the Tomb of Pope Sixtus IV by Antonio del Pollaiolo. Finally, we will visit the Caves of the Vatican (entrance from a pillar of the dome). Here, we find the remains of the ancient Costantinian Basilica and the tombs of many pontiffs.

Statue of St. Peter

the vatican city

Raphael, Transfiguration

The Vatican Museums

Raphael,
Madonna of
Foligno

The Vatican Palaces, enormous constructions with over 1400 rooms, host the precious Vatican Museums. A collection of antiquities, the most outstanding in the world, is gathered in the Pio Clementino Museum and the Chiaramonti Museum. However, the great Italian and European collection of paintings is kept in the fifteen rooms of the Vatican Picture-Gallery built by Luca Beltrami for Pope Pius XI.

In the ancient Roman Museum, enriched by Julius II in the 16th century, there are many works of art, among which the Laocoön. It represents the Trojan priest with his two sons being crushed to death by snakes as a penalty for warning the Trojans against the wooden horse. Of uncertain date – it may be a Hellenistic sculpture – it was found in 1506 in the "Domus Aurea". It depicts human pain and moral suffering with great pathos. The admirable Belvedere Torso, perhaps representing Hercules, was sculptured at the end of the 1st century BC. It was found in the 15th century and was studied extensively by Michelangelo. The Apollo of Belvedere is a Roman copy of a Greek work of art from the 4th century BC. Other works of art are the Augustus of the Prima Porta, a Roman statue. Especially admirable are the bas-relief of the cuirass and the Sleeping Ariadne, where Ariadne, abandoned by Thesius, sleeps in a affected pose. The drapery is typical of Hellenistic sculpture, of which this is a Roman copy.

Do not miss the Wounded Amazon (a copy of Phidias, 500 BC) and the Apoxyomenos (athlete scraping himself with a strigil), an original bronze by Lysippus, and the Doryphorus (spear carrier) a copy by Polycletus.

In the Vatican Picture-Gallery the development of art can be followed through the centuries. Beginning with the Stefaneschi polyptych by Giotto (1300 AD), the splendid Angel Musician by Melozzo da Forlì (a golden halo, lapislazuli sky) and, by the same artist, Sixtus IV and Platina.

The latter is a fresco where the Pope and his nephew (the future Julius II) stand with the Humanist called Platina. Admirable are: the Madonna and Child by Pinturicchio and the St. Benedict by Perugino (1495). By Raphael are the admirable: Madonna of Foligno, commissioned as a thanks offering to the Virgin, one of Raphael's first works completed in Rome in 1512, and the Transfiguration where Christ, bathed in supernatural light, arises supported by Moses and the prophet Elijah, while the apostles lie terrorised on the ground. This admirable work was given new splendour after its recent restoration.

The museum also hosts the unfinished but beautiful Saint Jerome by Leonardo, the Pietà by Giovanni Bellini and works of art of Van Dyck , Pietro da Cortona, Poussin, Titian and the splendid Deposition (1604) by Caravaggio.

Caravaggio,
Deposition

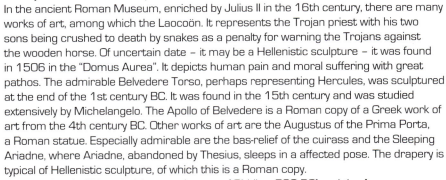

The Laocoön group

Raphael's rooms

In 1508 Pope Julius II wanted to finish the decorations of his apartments, started by Signorelli and Piero della Francesca but interrupted shortly after. Therefore, he entrusted the work to Raphael, a young artist whose genius has been compared to that of Leonardo and Michelangelo.

Dispute over the Eucharist

The Parnassus

The most beautiful room painted by Raphael is, perhaps, the Stanza della Segnatura, based on a complex programme in which theological, philosophical and political ideas are expressed through allegories. This is how the Disputation over the Sacraments was conceived, a great religious and symbolic fresco. The Parnassus is a fresco where Apollo is playing a violin among the Muses (here represented for the first time since antiquity) and a crowd of poets such as Alcaeus, Corinna, Petrarch, Anacreon, Ennius and the lonely Sappho (the only one not wearing a laurel wreath) as well as a group with Dante, Homer, Virgil and on the other side more poets: Pindar, Sannazzaro, Horace, Propertius, Tibullus, Catullus, Ovid and at the centre Ariosto. It is a great fresco celebrating poetry and beauty. Splendid, and probably the best known painting, is the so-called School of Athens an allegory of ancient philosophy as anticipator of Christianity. Then, the Stanza dell'Incendio, so-called because it depicts Pope Leo IV miraculously putting out a fire. Lastly, the Stanza di Costantino and the Stanza di Eliodoro of which the last painting is the Expulsion of Eliodorus from the Temple (standing to one side of the papal throne, dressed in a long black robe is Raphael – a self-portrait).

Stanza dell'incendio di Borgo

the vatican city

The Sistine Chapel

The Chapel (40,23 metres long, 20,70 metres high and 13,41 metres wide) was built at the end of the 15th century by Giovannino de' Dolci, in imitation of Noah's Ark. The walls were frescoed with twelve paintings (on the left scenes from the Life of Moses, on the right scenes from the Life of Jesus) by such artists as: Perugino, Pinturicchio, Botticelli, Signorelli and Ghirlandaio. However the greatest masterpieces of them all remain the frescoes of the vaults, painted by Michelangelo for Pope Julius II between 1508 and 1512 and the admirable and terrible Last Judgement painted for Pope Paul III around 1540.

Admirable are the decorative figures and biblical scenes which crowd the frescoes of the vault, a gigantic work that Michelangelo executed alone and in an extremely uncomfortable position. Powerful nude figures, assuming a variety of poses, separate and frame the paintings that contain scenes developing the great iconographic theme that goes from Creation and Original Sin to Redemption.

In the Creation of Adam the divine finger is almost united to that of the first man in whom God instils life. Admirable are: God separating light from darkness, The creation of the sun and the moon, The separation of earth and water, The creation of Eve, Original sin, and the well-known and dramatic Expulsion from Paradise, The story of Cain and Abel, The Flood, The drunkenness of Noah.

The powerful figures of the seven prophets and of the five sibyls frame the sides of this grandiose work of art. Perhaps even more famous is the huge outstanding Last Judgment on the altar wall. The scene is unique, made up of three hundred and ninety one figures surrounding Christ the Judge: near and above Him are the elect who rise at the sound of the trumpets, while below the damned are being led to hell by Charon and Minos.

Almost all the figures are naked and of great beauty while the whole is composed of hundreds of expressive scenes that circulate like a vortex, at once solemn and arresting. Rarely before has a work of art been able to express Man's dramatic destiny with such intensity.

❮❮ ... the visit goes on

The visit to the Vatican Palaces has other surprises in store: the Gallery of the Geographical Maps, the Gallery of the Tapestries, the Gallery of the Candelabras and The Hall of the Biga (because it exhibits a biga from the 1st century BC). ❯❯

the vatican city

NAPLES

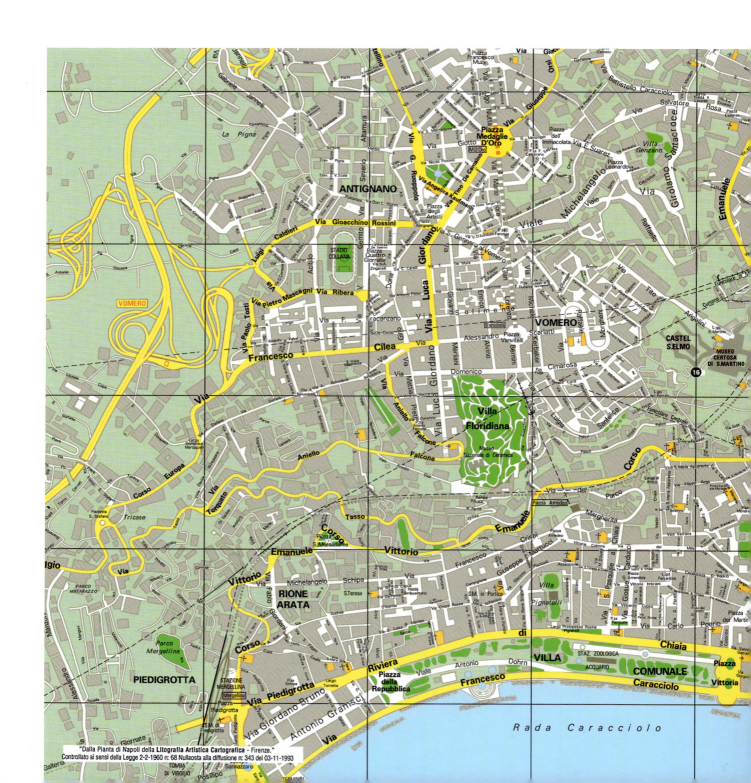

SCALA 1 : 10.000

0   50 100   200   300   400

1 cm = 100 m

1 - Museo Archeologico Nazionale
2 - Duomo
3 - Chiesa di S.Caterina a Formiello
4 - Porta Capuana
5 - Porta Nolana
6 - Chiesa di S.Maria del Carmine
7 - Chiesa di S.Lorenzo Maggiore
8 - Chiesa di S.Domenico Maggiore

9 - Chiesa di Gesù Nuovo
10 - Chiesa di S.Chiara
11 - Municipio
12 - Monumento a Vittorio Emanuele II
13 - Maschio Angioino
14 - Teatro S.Carlo
15 - Palazzo Reale
16 - Castel S.Elmo e Museo di S.Martino

historical background

Eumulo Favelo was the first Greek general to set foot, or rather to be shipwrecked, on the shores of the future Naples, at the beginning of the 11th century BC. Others say that the siren Partenope committed suicide where Castel dell'Ovo now stands. One thing is certain, Naples is of Greek origin and originated as a settlement near the present island of Ischia. In 470 BC the Cumans founded the real Naples where one of their commercial centres already existed: Neapolis, meaning "the new city". Temples and theatres were built and became, like Taranto and Cumae, one of the important centres of Magna Grecia.

The Roman emperor Tiberius owned a villa on Capri, as did later Caligola and Claudius. Cicero and Horacius wrote here. Pliny the Elder and Virgil settled in what is now Mergellina. During the Middle Ages, Naples was a bone of contention between the Western Empire and Byzantium, that conquered it; it was also a possible prey for many barbarians. Naples rebelled against the Eastern Empire in 615 AD and with the consent of Byzantium it became a relatively autonomous dukedom.

In 1137 the duke Sergio was forced to submit to the Norman king Roger II of Altavilla. The Normans came from distant Scandinavian countries and conquered the south of Italy; Roger II had himself proclaimed "king of Sicily and Italy". On the death of Tancredi the south of Italy came under the rule of other foreigners, the Swabians. The great glory of this dynasty was what the wise Frederick II called "the splendour of the world". He was a great military leader and intellectual. He founded a university in Naples that for centuries was one of the most important in Europe. On the death of Frederick, Naples, during years of great agitation, passed frequently from Swabian to Papal rule. The Pope founded in Naples the first municipal system headed by a podestà, the first being Riccardo Filangieri. This regime lasted until Charles d'Anjou, brother to the king of France, came to Italy at the request of the Pope and took over the rule of the south of Italy.

After it had been taken over by the Anjou, Naples knew a period of unprecedented prosperity. Churches and monuments were built, commerce and crafts flourished and it became a great European metropolis, like Paris, especially as the capital of the kingdom, Palermo, was transferred from Sicily to Naples. Charles II enlarged and renovated the Castel dell'Ovo and the Maschio Angioino by Pietro Cavallini and Montano d'Arezzo. Then Robert d'Anjou came to the throne and he became a legendary figure because of his foresight (Santa Chiara, San Lorenzo, San Paolo Maggiore, San Domenico Maggiore and the Cathedral built on a pre-existing early Christian church). In the early 14th century the poet Petrarch came to Naples in order to be crowned poet laureate by Robert d'Anjou. Under his rule Giotto and Tino di Camaino also sojourned in Naples. The crown passed to the house of Aragon. Under their rule Naples enjoyed an era of economic prosperity and refinement. In spite of earthquakes and periodic outbreaks of the plague – a too frequent occurrence in Naples – the Accademia Pontaniana was founded. Here were gathered men like Jacopo Sannazzaro and Giovanni Pontano, and Masuccio from Salerno, author of the "Novellino". And the city witnessed a rich flowering of such works of art as Sant'Anna of the Lombardi and the magnificent Triumphal Arch.

Now followed a long, sad period in the history of Naples lasting for two centuries (1503-1707); it fell under Spanish dominion and was badly governed by the Spanish viceroys. The Neapolitans frequently rebelled; in the 16th century against the dreaded Inquisition, in the 17th century there was a serious revolt against the Spanish lead by the legendary Masaniello. To political oppression leading to misery and economic ruin were added repeated earthquakes and eruptions of Vesuvius.

Nevertheless, intellectual and artistic expansion continued at a great pace: in literature there were Torquato Tasso and Giovanbattista Basile and the elegant Gianbattista Marino; in art the painters Luca Giordano and Mattia Preti excelled; Caravaggio also worked here; the Royal Palace, the Church of Gesù and the Chartreuse of St. Martin were built. The long Bourbon rule started in 1734 when Charles of Bourbon came to the throne. For many reasons their rule is not to be despised. It ended in 1860 when Naples became part of the kingdom of Italy.

There have been many negative criticisms of the Bourbon rule, but modern historians have reevaluated it. Charles I, the first king, inaugurated many reforms. He introduced a register of landed property, modernised the port, founded an efficient merchant navy and enriched the capital with masterpieces such as The Royal Palace of Capodimonte, the Royal Palace of Caserta entrusted to Vanvitelli (judged

worthy of Versailles), the Royal Villa of Portici. He subsequently founded the soon to be legendary porcelain factory of Capodimonte and he had the San Carlo Theatre built which became one of the musical centres of Europe. Soon, with composers such as Alessandro Scarlatti and Giovanbattista Pergolesi ("La serva padrona") and later Giovanni Paisiello and Domenico Cimarosa, the Neapolitan School enjoyed international prestige.

In 1789 the effects of the French Revolution reached Naples. Struggles and uprisings began which only ended with the Risorgimento (the movement to unite Italy). Then Napoleon ordered the occupation of Naples in 1799 and proclaimed the Partenopean Republic, soon to be defeated in a blood bath and through acts of vengeance by the troops lead by Cardinal Ruffo di Calabria. (The patriots Mario Pagano and Domenico Cirillo were shot and the English admiral Nelson joined the Neapolitan admiral Francesco Caracciolo in an anti-French coalition.) The Bourbons were restored very rapidly, but were dethroned again by Napoleon, and in their place he made his brother Joseph king of the south of Italy, and so the French re-occupied Naples. After Joseph who had ruled as an enlightened monarch – his reign saw the founding of the Botanical Gardens and the Conservatory of Music – another Frenchman, Joseph Murat, came to the throne but he was deposed after the Congress of Vienna to be replaced by the legitimate Bourbon. Ferdinand, back on the throne, passed the statute that regulated the whole kingdom of the Two Sicilies and signed a concordat with the Church by which all church lands were restored to the Church. He also launched a new set of laws deemed by historians to be the most advanced in Europe. Meanwhile, new monuments were being added to Naples: Piazza del Plebiscito, the Church of San Francesco di Paola, the Villa Floridiana al Vomero, the Astronomical Observatory of Capodimonte. His successors, Francesco I and Ferdinand II, ruled by alternating illusions, concessions and brutal repressions (the patriots Poerio, Settembrini and Spaventa paid dearly for their patriotism in harsh prisons). Ferdinand died in 1859, a year before the unification of Italy, when Naples was as yet one of the intellectual leaders of Europe. Naples was the first in Italy to enjoy gas light, to have a railway, to install telegraph lines. Nor can the leading role of the Neapolitan theatre – from Edoardo Scarpetta to Eduardo de Filippo – during the first half of the 19th century, be forgotten, nor the famous Neapolitan songs and composers such as the great Donizetti.

Naples joined the newly-united Kingdom of Italy. Historians all agree, in varying degrees, that Italy neither then nor later treated Naples well. No longer a capital, but a provincial town, it sank into a long period of decadence, neglected by Rome and afflicted either with the Camorra (a criminal group, although it started as a means of helping the impoverished plebs), or the "brigantaggio", a complex phenomenon of criminals opposed to the state. Many southern industries were dismantled, internal tolls were multiplied, the old sore, the "latifondo" (vast estates), worsened. The decadence of Naples continued under Fascism although the south sought a way out to increase trade and commerce, hence the Mostra d'Oltremare and the Fiera del Levante. The Neapolitans suffered greatly during World War II from the allied bombings, but they became great heroes during the "four days of Naples" when they rose against the atrocities of the Nazis.

During the years following the war, the inadequate governments failed to restitute to Naples the position that was traditionally hers. It is only during the last years that there has been a tendency to reverse this policy. Their increasing confidence helps to encourage social and economic renewal. There is at the same time a definite increase in the amount of visitors each year to Naples.

The squares

If you want to discover the type of people who live in a town... its squares and streets are usually the most revealing places. This is particularly true of Naples where the climate and landscape bring out the best in the Neapolitan. Passionate, extrovert, fond of company, a natural actor, he is always willing to play a role, be it comic or tragic. Streets and squares truly reflect the adventure called Naples. Our brief visit will only permit us to observe the most characteristic and renowned squares and streets of the town. There are many omissions. The visitor will discover these for himself as he strolls through the city.

Piazza Plebiscito

The "Heart of Naples", Piazza Plebiscito, the biggest square in the city, is located where once were found the ancient Greek walls and the Lucillian "castrum" (fortress); it later became the site of churches and convents. Today it is bounded by the magnificent Royal Palace (the front is 169 metres long) and, on the opposite side, by the neo-classic church of San Francesco di Paola. The Royal Palace belongs to the 18th century; it was ordered by a Spanish viceroy, based on plans by Domenico Fontana (later Vanvitelli worked on it). The church is 19th century, and was built by order of Ferdinand I by Pietro Bianchi in 1836. There is a small portico in front of its circular base. On opposite sides of the square stand two buildings, Palazzo Salerno and Palazzo della Prefettura, which are stylistically similar. Palazzo Salerno, begun in 1775, was restructured many times in order to meet the needs of the Bourbon ministers, who met there until 1825. Later its façade was made to conform to that of the neo-classic building facing it, the Palace of the Prefettura, which was built around 1815 by Leopoldo Laperuta and which

Piazza Plebiscito, at night

has on the ground floor the renowned Café Gambrinus, one of the oldest, most famous and most patronised cafés of Naples (another café in the same piazza, the Café Tripoli, formerly the Turkish Café, was closed in 1932). Two equestrian monuments stand side by side in the square: the statues of Charles III and Ferdinand IV of Bourbon are by Antonio Canova, while the figure of King Ferdinand is by Antonio Calì. The beautiful Fountain of the Immacolatella (see Fountains of Naples) is admirable. Plebiscite Square has always been the centre of Naples, here where once carousels, tournaments, and also official weddings took place. On major occasions food, cheese, poultry and meat were distributed to the people as an act of goodwill on the part of the rulers. Joachim Murat planned the construction of a large amphitheatre, whose terraces were dug in the nearby hill of Pizzofalcone; the whole work was named Murat Forum.

Piazza Dante

Piazza Dante, looking on to the Via Toledo, received its final form in the middle of the 1700's, earlier than Piazza Plebiscito. Called formerly Piazza del Mercatiello (of the little market) because of the market that was held there from the end of the 1500's, the square was rearranged at the order of Charles of Bourbon by Luigi Vanvitelli in 1757. After the unification of Italy it was dedicated to the poet Dante Alighieri, whose statue, a work of Tito Angelini (1872), stands in the centre. Vanvitelli planned the large exedra that included in its northern part Port'Alba (built in 1625, later redesigned) and was to have in its centre a big opening with an equestrian monument to Charles (never built) followed by an extended semicircular space subdivided into 3 files of columns and pilasters (nowadays the whole complex houses a school). In front of it the visitor can see the convent and the Church of San Domenico Soriano, completed at the middle of the 16th century. The beautiful dome frescoed by Mattia Preti, and the remarkable high altar of multicoloured marble are noteworthy. Worth seeing are the paintings by Gerolamo Imparato and Luca Giordano. The monastic complex is now used as offices. Nearby is the extraordinary Palace of Ruffo di Bagnara, erected around 1660 by Carlo Fontana. Not far from here is the convent of Santa Maria del Caravaggio, founded by the Scolopian Fathers in 1627. Earlier it was a school for poor children, then it was transformed at the end of the 1700's by Giovan Battista Nauclerio (in one chapel is the Death of St. Joseph, ascribed to Solimera).

Piazza del Municipio

The vast and evocative Town Hall Square is dominated by the imposing Castel Nuovo (New Castle) or Maschio Angioino. After having admired the view of Vesuvius and breathed the air of the Harbour with its shipping-station, here and in the immediate surroundings we seem to hear the vibration of the notes coming from the Merchant Theatre (1778, project of Francesco Securo) with its restructured 19th c. façade. Going round the monument of Victor Immanuel II in the middle of the square, and passing the beautiful gardens, we find the Town Hall Palace or St. James. This was formerly the office of the Bourbon ministers, built at the beginning of the 1800's and which assimilated (in 1825) the façade of the beautiful Church of San Giacomo degli Spagnoli, built in 1540 at the behest of the Spaniards. With its 3 aisles the church retains a 16th c. look. Noteworthy are the marble tombs and the interesting paintings, among which those of Luca Giordano.

Piazza San Domenico Maggiore

Here, near various imposing buildings, the medieval Church of San Domenico Maggiore and, in its centre, the curious spire erected in 1656 to commemorate the end of the plague, on which worked Cosimo Fonzago, Francesco Antonio Picchiatti and Domenico Antonio Vaccaro. On the left of the square is the entrance to the Palace of Antonelli Petrucci, a frequently retouched 15th c. building. In front of the church-apse, there is the Palace of the dukes of Casacalenda, of 18th c. restructured by Luigi Vanvitelli. There are more buildings to see, in particular Palazzo Sansevero with its round-arched Portal with rusticated half columns by Vitale Finelli, and Palazzo Corigliano, of the 16th c. (restructured many times before the 19th c.).

Church of San Domenico
Maggiore, interior

The sea-promenade

Starting from the gorgeous Via Parthenope we walk down the beautiful Via Caracciolo along which we find, among many other green gardens, the Villa Comunale; in its park are the Zoological Station, centre of international studies, and the well-known large Aquarium. Here begins the Mergellina, the famous bay that forms part of the Gulf, where you find the vivid and crowded Sannazzaro Harbour. From Via Mergellina the funicular goes up to the historic hill of Posillipo (you can also get there by walking along Via Posillipo). Do not miss Posillipo Park, from whose Belvedere one can take in the whole coast. Going back to Via Mergellina we now walk towards Piedigrotta, for ages a source of songs, music, and of the Neapolitan soul which shows itself particularly on the occasion of the celebration of the Madonna di Piedigrotta (September 7 and 8). Not far from here – near the Church of Santa Maria di Piedigrotta, two renowned tombs have to be visited: the first is the tomb of Giacomo Leopardi, under a classic monument – a half-column with an ionic capital. Leopardi died in Naples in 1837 and was first buried in San Vitale in Fuorigrotta.

The second tomb belongs to the Latin poet Virgil: the presumed remains of the poet, who lived in Naples in a villa, a gift of the philosopher Siron, are in the Virgilian Park. The tomb, typical of Roman monuments, is a cubic space surmounted by a cylinder covered with calcareous slabs. The interior, with its barrel vault, has ten niches.

The new quarter of Fuorigrotta begins beyond Virgilian Park. From here, back to the Piazza della Repubblica, we walk along the Riviera of Chiaia and, passing a couple of beautiful churches, reach the Pignatelli Museum and the Museum of the Coaches (see the chapter on museums).

Another possible tour starts from Piazza Trento e Trieste, arriving at Piazza Dante down the very famous Toledo Street, where we find the historic Church of Sant'Anna dei Lombardi (see the chapter on churches), the magnificent Church of the Gesù Nuovo (same chapter) and finally the Church and the Monastery of Santa Chiara (again see the chapter on churches), so that history and art interweave through an extraordinary series of images and views, exactly as is Naples, beautiful and ancient.

Castles and Fortresses

Maschio Angioino or New Castle

Imposing and solemn, it rises in front of the Piazza Municipio with its five towers and its bright Triumphal Arch. It got its name from Charles I of Anjou, who had it built as a royal residence in 1279. The Maschio is connected to famous events, such as the "great refusal" by pope Celestine V, the election of Boniface VIII, Giotto's visit, who produced there various frescoes (now lost), the visit of the poet Petrarch. Enriched by the addition of the Palatine Chapel thanks to Charles II, the Castle was transformed by the Aragonese, particularly by King Alphonso, who made of it at the same time a powerful fortress and a comfortable residence, using such Catalan architects as Ptats, Vila Sclar, Gomar. Inside, beyond the courtyard, we find the splendid Palatine Chapel or Chapel of Santa Barbara: it is a marvellous example of Gothic art, the only surviving witness, here, of the Angevin age. It has a square base, cross-vault and high windows and was frescoed by Giotto (the frescoes are unfortunately lost). If we go further, we come to the famous Hall of the Barons (today the meeting-place of Naples' city council). Planned by Sagrera, with a square base and an octagonal vault, the hall earned its fame because of the conspiracy of the feudal barons (hence the name) against the king, who collected them here by a stratagem and had them killed. Under the arcade is stored the big Bronze Door of the Castle, with its bas-reliefs where a cannon-ball had run into it during an unknown battle or siege. The annexed Civic Museum has interesting frescoes from the 14th century, splendid tabernacles, silver, as well as sculptures by Vincenzo Gemito.

The triumphal Arch
King Alphonso's entry into Naples

One of the most remarkable monuments of the southern Renaissance, this Triumphal Arch is in reality a curious historic forgery. In fact, it illustrates the triumphal entry of Alphonso of Aragon into Naples, after he conquered and dethroned René of Anjou. King Alphonso is portrayed in the central bas-relief with crown, mantel, and, in his hand, globe and sceptre, as symbols of power. In reality King Alphonso, in order to defeat the resisting D'Anjou, had to use the expedient of entering the town first; only then could Alphonso transform Castel Nuovo from a fortress into a royal residence, although he retained as many as five watchtowers. The four-levelled Triumphal Arch, built in marble and standing between the watchtowers, is the work of various artists, mainly Tuscan, among whom Francesco Laurana, Isaia da Pisa, Paolo Romano and also the Spaniard Pere Joan. The basal arch in Roman style is inserted between Corinthian columns. It is surmounted by the magnificent relief of the Triumph; over it there is a second arch between Doric columns, that was originally meant to hold Alphonso's statue. At an even higher level there are the four statues of the cardinal virtues, then the figures of two personified rivers and finally, at the summit, the statue of St. Michael the Archangel. The work celebrates Alphonso of Aragon's elaborate entry strategy into Naples (26th of February 1443), thus emulating similar monuments of Roman triumphs, although in a more agreeable Renaissance key.

The monumental fountains
beautiful, glorious… well-travelled

The many large freshwater fountains dating mainly from the 17th century are the glory of Naples. They are "well-travelled" as almost none of them are in their original place; they were displaced thanks, no doubt, to the extravagance of some viceroy. The first on the list is the gorgeous Fountain of Medina (in Bovio square), a late 16th century monument showing Neptune and satyrs, on which artists such as

Domenico D'Auria, Pietro Bernini and Michelangelo Naccherino worked. A hundred years later Cosimo Fonzago added balustrades and steps which emphasised its verticality. It was moved to its present place only at the end of the 19th century. Perhaps the most beautiful fountain in Naples is the three arched Fountain of the Immacolatella (1601) in white and grey marble. Its Tritons and Caryatids, as well as 3 superb marble coat-of-arms distinguish the whole work. Then there is the curious Fountain of Sebeto (between Posillipo and Mergellina), a work of Cosimo Fonzago, who was inspired by Michelangelo's gigantism, especially in the illustration of the bearded giant, who is supposed to represent the Sebeto river, nowadays of little importance. In the Villa Comunale, close to each other, are the splendid Fountain of the Rape of Europe, built in 1798 by Angelo Viva, and the more complex and airy Fountain of Santa Lucia (1606), signed by Michelangelo Naccherino and Tommaso Montani. The latter is distinctive because of its big central arch and the mythological bas-reliefs at the sides. The Fountain of the Papparelle, built by Sammartino, had at its summit first the Siren of Parthenope, then the Farnese Bull. Stripped of its ornaments, it was then "embellished" by the Neapolitans, who supplied the basin with living ducks (hence its name). Noteworthy is its elegant basin supported by lions. Finally in the square of the same name is the characteristic Fountain of Monteoliveto, by D.A. Cafaro (1668) at whose summit the statue of King Charles II as a child looks towards a spot where, so Neapolitans say, a treasure is buried.

Castel dell'Ovo

A very ancient Norman stronghold in front of the Santa Lucia harbour, Castel dell'Ovo was built by King Roger II on a pre-existent Roman building (its beautiful columns are still visible), presumably the villa of the famous Roman patrician Lucius Lucullus. Frederic II fortified it with towers, Charles I of Anjou made it as his royal residence. Robert of Anjou decided to build new towers and around the end of the 14th century the imposing building gained a new structure. Castel dell'Ovo (Egg Castle) received its name –according to the legend– because the poet and wizard Virgil buried in its depths a magic egg, which, if broken, was to bring bad luck to the town. The Castle witnessed important events of Naples' history: Corradino of Swabia and later Tommaso Campanella were here imprisoned; Masaniello's revolt started here and the ephemeral Parthenope Republic of 1799 was centred here.

Inside, Castel dell'Ovo still retains Norman towers, the very ancient Chiesetta di San Salvatore (the small church of S.S.), the cells of a hermit convent and, in the royal apartments, a big hall with the wonderful Roman columns of Lucullus' villa. Note the remarkable Gothic and Catalan open galleries. Castel dell'Ovo was restructured in 1975 and has today an interesting prehistoric museum organised by the CAI. The museum contains over 4000 objects from the agricultural, artisan and domestic spheres of primitive ages, from 70,000 to 3,000 years BC, following precise chronological criteria, it also has a large ethnographic section.

Castel Sant'Elmo

Visible from every part of town, Castel Sant'Elmo, rising on top of St. Martin's hill, is a fortress built during the time of King Robert of Anjou (1329). On the powerful walls protected by a moat, the famous Tino da Camaino erected two square towers (demolished at the end of the fifteenth century). In 1538, by the order of the Spanish viceroy, the Castle was transformed by the military architect Pedro Luis Scrivà, who erected a building with a star-shaped base and big pointed protruding spurs, most likely following the suggestion of Francesco di Giorgio Martini, guest of the king of Naples at the end of the 1400's. This castle has always played a prominent part of the town's history, a symbol of its protective power throughout the centuries. Often destroyedonce even by lightning- it has been in turn a prison (for Tommaso Campanella and, later, for Luisa San Felice), a residence and a drillground. Walking through the old prisons, the endless corridors, the steps, the huge square and the church of Sant'Elmo, is a very evocative experience. From almost every corner you can enjoy a magnificent view of Naples.

The Umberto Gallery
the livingroom of Naples

At the end of the last century Naples decided to have its very own Gallery, as did many European metropolitan centres, among them Milan just 20 years previously. It was, in fact, built in 1887 right in the middle of the town amongst famous buildings and churches (this area had first to be

cleared of its entangled lanes that were a nest of mainly criminal activity). The gallery was designed by the engineer Emanuele Rocco and the architects Antonio Curri and Ernesto di Mauro. In a vast and protected urban area, with business functions enhanced by its monumentality in pure belle-époque style, the Gallery has the following features: it is 147 metres long, 15 metres wide, 34,5 metres high, and the dome is 57 metres high. Richly decorated in neo-Renaissance style, the Gallery has a glass-steel covering, an octagonal cross-vault plan, four exit arms, a multicoloured marble floor with the Zodiac and a compass (Venetian mosaic) in its centre. This comfortable and warm Umbertine monument immediately became the favourite meeting place of Neapolitan high society, and especially of artists and musicians of the nearby Salone Margherita, haunt of pleasure seekers. D'Annunzio, Salvatore di Giacomo, Eduardo Scarfoglio, Ferdinando Russo were regular visitors here. Today it remains a relic of the past, but is also still the pulse of a town that loves to congregate out of doors. »

The Churches

Neapolitan churches are simultaneously a pilgrimage and an artistic experience.
Unfortunately far too many churches (and the works of art which are kept in them) remain closed to the public, because of restoration or simply because they have been forgotten by all.
There is, in short, a large hidden Naples, that is only now awakening from a long slumber, thanks to a new civic involvement on the part of the neapolitans and the initiative of the mayor.

The Cathedral

The Cathedral is the religious heart of Naples and the guardian of the relics of the patron San Gennaro, much loved by the Neapolitans. It was built during the reigns of Charles II of Anjou and his son Robert, between the 13th and the 14th centuries, undergoing many adjustments and modifications with the passage of time. In this very place were the ancient basilicas of Santa Restituta (4th century) and Santa Stefania (5th century). The latter was destroyed and a part of the former was included as one of the chapels in the present Cathedral. The Cathedral's interior was enriched by stuccoes at the end of the 1600's; it has now a very recent neo-Gothic façade by Enrico Alvino (end of the last century), incorporating the three original Gothic portals by Antonio Baboccio.
In the central portal there is an outstanding Madonna with Child by Tino da Camaino.
The interior is in the shape of a Latin cross. It has three aisles and is about 100 metres long, and around the big pilasters 110 granite columns crowd together. A wonderful coffered ceiling covers the central aisle. At the base of the Baptismal Font is a precious antique Greek object.
The Chapel of San Gennaro, centre of the Cathedral and almost a church within a church, will be discussed separately. The visitor can now turn to the magnificent Chapel of Santa Restituta and to the Baptistery, perhaps the oldest early Christian baptistery in the Western world.
The Chapel of Santa Restituta contains traces of the ancient early Christian basilica, the first cathedral of Naples, built perhaps by the emperor Constantine on top of a pagan temple.

 naples

Chapel of San Gennaro

Be sure to visit the Minutolo Chapel in the Cathedral, with its frescoes from the third and fourth centuries, the Tomb of Cardinal Minutolo, and the gorgeous mosaic pavement. See also the Bracaccio Chapel and the Tocco Chapel, with precious 4th century frescoes by Pietro Cavallini.

❰❰ San Gennaro, salvation of Naples
a six hundred year old miracle

If Vesuvius is Naples' threat, San Gennaro has been for centuries its salvation. Few towns in the world show such long-lasting and passionate attachment to its own patron saint, an attachment sanctioned by a miracle that repeats itself twice a year (the liquefying of the saint's blood contained in an ampulla, in front of the praying population): this happens on September 19th and on the Saturday preceding the first Sunday of May. St. Gennaro, bishop of Benevento, was

beheaded in 305 at Pozzuoli during Diocletian's persecution. In 472, following a violent eruption of Vesuvius, Neapolitans chose Gennaro as their patron saint: his remains were moved from Benevento to Montevergine and now finally rest in the Cathedral in Naples. Neapolitans bestow upon St. Gennaro an almost idolatrous veneration, which nothing can perturb and which expresses itself in daily practices as well as in impressive processions at recurrent celebrations, during which the saint's bust, dressed in sacred vestments, is paraded in front of the enthusiastic faithful. St. Gennaro's Chapel, with the annexed "Treasury of St. Gennaro" containing thousands of precious objects given by the faithful, was built in the Cathedral between 1608 and 1637 and is a gorgeous example of the Neapolitan Baroque. For its construction the queen regent offered the outstanding sum of 30,000 scudi, but the Neapolitans refused, wishing the entire financing to come from the population. The entrance to the Chapel is enriched by a magnificent gilded bronze gate by Cosimo Fanzago. The interior surmounted by a dome is decorated with great Baroque paintings by Domenichino, Giuseppe Ribera (St. Gennaro emerging unscathed from a furnace), and Luca Giordano. There is a splendid bust of the saint (together with 50 other busts) in gilded silver, the work of French artists. In the Chapel there are the ampullas containing the saint's blood. From the presbytery there is access to the crypt, where the saint's bones are kept. ❱❱

Church of Santa Maria Donnaregina

Actually two churches bear this name, a splendid one from the 14th century, and a second one (called the new church), in the Baroque style, that is partially connected with the first one. The second church, built around 1600 and planned by Giovanni Guarino, has in its vault frescoes by Francesco de Benedectis. Noteworthy is the Assumption of the Virgin (1654). The hand of Solimena can be identified in the frescoes on the choir, high altar and door of the tabernacle. Distinctive and elegant is the iron gridwork of the chapels, which are surmounted by the gilded gratings of the women's galleries. The real masterpiece is, however, the (old) Church of Santa Maria Donnaregina from the 14th century, an original monument of Italian Gothic art. Among its works, not to be missed is the Tomb of Queen Mary of Hungary, a splendid 14th century piece by Tino da Camaino. There are also the precious frescoes featuring a pictorial cycle of the early 1300's with scenes from the Life of Christ and the Apostles (strong influence of Giotto). Also influenced by Giotto are the frescoes of the Loffredo Chapel and the Choir. Today this church, evocative because of its magical and archaic spaces, is the centre of the School for Specialisation in Monumental Restoration of the Faculty of Architecture of Naples.

Church of St. John of Carbonara

This church, begun in 1343, is one of the most beautiful in Naples. We enter it via a particularly splendid elliptic double flight of stairs, built by Ferdinando Sanfelice in 1708. The imposing funeral monument to Ladislaus of Durazzo (died 1414), a king about whom the historians have expressed differing opinions, is the main focus of this visit.

The monument, commissioned by his sister Jane II, is 18 metres high, occupies a whole wall and shows a superb range of allegoric statues by Marco and Andrea da Firenze. Going through the space under an architrave, between the caryatids of the monument, we reach the Caracciolo del Sole Chapel, which hosts the Sepulchre of Ser Gianni Caracciolo built in 1432 and probably also by Andrea da Firenze. Noteworthy are the majolica floor and the frescoes on the walls by Leonardo da Besozzo and Perinetto da Benevento, with Stories of the Virgin Mary and Lives of the Hermits. Beautiful and valuable is also the Caracciolo di Vito Chapel (1517) on a circular plan sketched by Tommaso Malvito, with sculptures of Bartolomeo Ordez and Diego de Siloe.

Last but not least there is the magnificent monument Miroballo (by Malvito and Jacopo della Pila). A final visit should be paid to the superb Crucifixion by Vasari in the Chapel of Antonio Seripando.

Church and Cloister of Santa Chiara

In August 1943 a terrible air-raid destroyed most of the Santa Chiara complex, which was perhaps the greatest example of Gothic architecture in Naples. Only the walls and façade remain, with the big rose-window and the portal.

The disaster necessitated careful reconstruction; during the reconstruction the Baroque superstructures, which at the middle of the 1700's had distorted the pure Gothic profile of the building, were stripped away. Unfortunately Giotto's invaluable paintings in the church and choir were lost. Santa Chiara was built by order of Robert of Anjou and his wife Sancia as a court chapel, together with a Franciscan convent and a cloister for the Clarisse nuns (the first example of female and male orders cohabiting). The church was built around 1310 on the plan of Gagliardo Primario following the strict rules of Franciscan poverty: only one aisle (82 metres long and 45 metres high) with 10 chapels on each side. Even now its very simplicity is its most inspiring feature. The cloister adds further charm because of its older part (14th century) with frescoes by Bellisario Corenzio, Tintoretto's follower, and because of its 18th century part, beautifully tiled by the ceramists Donato and Giuseppe Massa. In 1739 an abbess built the cloister garden one sees today: a wonderful fusion of wisteria and white narcissus. The seats, partition walls and columns are decorated by the majolicas of Donato and Giuseppe Massa. The garden, by the way, was "rediscovered" through the writings of Benedetto Croce. The Church was an Angevin religious centre and the remains of their kings were brought there, first of all King Robert's, whose monumental sepulchre is the wonderful work of Giovanni and Pacio Bertini from Florence.

Tino da Camaino built the sepulchres of Mary of Valois and of Robert's son, Charles of Calabria. During the Bourbon era Sammartino built the funeral monument to Philip, son of Charles III (1777).

Cloister

Interior of the church of
Sant'Anna dei Lombardi

Church of Sant'Anna dei Lombardi

A splendid example of the Renaissance style in Naples, this church contains admirable works. It was begun in 1411 and consecrated to the Virgin of Monteoliveto, while the actual name derives from the Company of the Lombards which settled here in the 1700's.

The façade has a Gothic arch and the 15th century door was recently rebuilt. In the hall there is the sepulchre of Domenico Fontana; it is he who gave Naples so many of its works of art. Here too the Baroque shows its influence in an altar as well as in the side chapels which are certainly the most valuable parts of this church. In the Renaissance chapel of the Mastrogiudice family we can see the reliefs by Benedetto da Maiano. In the Tolosa Chapel the frescoes are by Giuliano da Maiano, and the four terracotta roundels are of the Della Robbia school.

Also worth seeing is the altar by Rossellino who worked with Benedetto da Maiano on the Funeral Monument to Mary of Aragon. Lament over the dead Christ in the Orilia Chapel by the 15th century artist Guido Mazzoni, is curious and evocative. It consists of eight terracotta statues of remarkable proportions (St. Joseph and Nicodemus were possibly modelled on Ferrante I and Alphonso of Aragon). In the sacristy and Chapel of the Assunta are paintings by Giorgio Vasari, which testify to the strong influence of the Florentine Renaissance in Naples.

Interior of the Cupola

Sacristy

Guido Mazzoni, Lament over the dead Christ (1492)

Church of San Lorenzo Maggiore

It is one of the greatest religious complexes (church and convent) in Naples and is of particular interest because of the overlapping styles from various times, from antique Greece to the 1700's. Here, so they say, Boccaccio met Fiammetta, and Petrarch himself would have visited in it. Here the Neapolitan people gathered to protest against the Inquisition in Naples (which was subsequently abolished). The church was commissioned by Charles I of Anjou in the mid-13th century, on the same spot where was once an early Christian basilica. From the actual cloister we come to important excavations containing Roman and Greek remains (amongst which a Roman street with shops and a market).

The Refectory Hall of the Franciscan Friars was the site of the Parliament in the Aragonese time (today it is the city record office). The 18th century façade is by Ferdinando Sanfelice, while the beautiful marble Portal with Gothic arch is a remnant of the Angevin period (1324). Noteworthy is the bell-tower dating from the 1500's, which replaced the older Angevin tower. The church has been modified many times, one of the reasons being the frequent earthquakes. Thanks to excellent restoration, the temple has today been transformed back to its Gothic structure, still preserving the most interesting Baroque innovations. Inside, to the right of the entrance there, is a remarkable wooden Crucifix of the 14th century. Some sepulchres follow: in the choir there is the Sepulchre of Catherine of Austria by the great Tino da Camaino. To the right, among the first chapels, there is the grand Sepulchre of Ludovico Aldomorisco, a 15th century work by Antonio Baboccio. Superb examples of 15th century work are the frescoes in the transept depicting the Nativity and the Death of the Virgin Mary. Four wonderful paintings by Mattia Preti, located in the Cappellone di Sant'Antonio (St. Anthony's Great Chapel), were painted three centuries later.

Church and Chartreuse of St. Martin

Built as a monastery in the 1300's, it underwent a radical transformation during the 1600's thanks to Cosimo Fanzago, whose work left its mark on Naples.

From the middle of the 1800's the Chartreuse has had a Museum with important exhibits, which will be discussed in our section about museums. For the moment the Church, the large and small cloister, and the beautiful gardens, will be discussed.

Charles of Anjou commissioned the Chartreuse in 1325 (one of the builders was Tino da Camaino).

The Catholic Counter-reformation brought substantial modifications by Antonio Bosio. During those years Fanzago contributed heavily as builder and decorator. Since 1886, after the expulsion of the Carthusian Friars, the complex has mainly been used as a museum.

The annexes are beautiful: the Cloister of the Procurators, the Refectory, the Gardens (with the Prior's orchard and the monks' vineyards) and the

Foreshortened
big cloister

Big Cloister. The latter is surrounded by a pleasant porch with eight statues on the balustrade (among them San Martino and San Bruno are the most significant), and with six medallions over the corner doors of the porch. Fanzago's Baroque elegance and talent is here at its best. The Cimiterino dei Monaci (Small Cemetery of the Monks) is worth a visit.

We now turn to the beautiful church. Past the 14th century porch, the only existent aisle offers an evocative sight: putti, rose-windows, statues, inlays, balustrades, columns, everything fits harmoniously in the architectural structure. The floor has splendid marble mosaics "alla certosina"; in the many side chapels there are works by Ribera, Battistello Caracciolo, Guido Reni, Massimo Stazione.

The high altar is surmounted by the precious Resurrection by Solimena, the temple's vault is frescoed by Giovanni Lanfranco (the Ascension); also noteworthy is the 17th century choir.

San Francesco di Paola

It is one of the newcomers and most magnificent and majestic churches of Naples.
Ferdinand of Bourbon commissioned it in the 1800's to the Luganese architect Pietro
Bianchi to fulfil a vow made before regaining his throne.
The church was built in neo-classic style, imitating the Roman Pantheon, with a circular
base; it was begun in 1816 and finished about 30 years later.
Inside is a rotunda corresponding to a dome 53 metres high, containing the oldest part of
the church.
The altar and tabernacle were transferred here from the Church of the Holy Apostles.
The altar, inlaid with lapislazuli and precious stones, was designed by Ferdinando Fuga
(1751); the 17th century tabernacle is by Grimaldi of Chieti. Among the most noticeable
paintings in the church is St. Francis of Paola resurrecting a child by Vincenzo Camuccini.
This large, original church contains a scansion of thirty four Corinthian columns
supporting the semi-spherical dome. Outside, the church almost resembles a
pagan temple with a majestic semispheric colonnade (taken from the Marat
Forum, an unrealised project of a Napoleonic sovereign), containing the
equestrian statues of Ferdinand I and Charles III of Bourbon. Both show the influence of
the great Canova.

naples

The Art of the Figurine Makers

the neapolitan devotion to the presepe (manger)

In Naples the "manger" is not only an object of pious devotion, but also an inspiration to artists. The art of making figurines started here two centuries ago. Sometimes it turned out to be a work of high quality, at other times it was but a naive folk-product. They also made an impressive

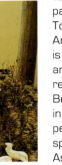

variety of figurines in terracotta where the Neapolitans are represented as paying homage to the Holy Family.

To understand what this "art of making mangers" is, visit San Gregorio Armeno Street between November and Christmas when the big figurine fair is held. Next to it is a market where bargains are found side by side with antique treasures. There is a museum near the Chartreuse of St. Martin renowned for its rare works, amongst which the Manger Cuciniello.

Begun in Umbria, so it seems, by the Franciscans, the manger in Naples, in the 1700's, developed theatrical connotations. Charles II of Bourbon personally had made a manger at his court. The custom of having a manger spread from the churches to the nobles and finally to the people.

As a form of devout religious expression, the Neapolitan manger is a world in miniature teeming with personages: from beggars to Moors, from butchers to peasants, from craftsmen of every kind to oyster-sellers; today there are also personages drawn from the news, politics and show business. So we may see the infant Jesus worshipped by Pulcinella, or maybe by the great Totò.

The sumptuous theatres of Naples

glory of Cimarosa, Paisiello, Bellini, Donizzetti, Rossini

Naples is full of theatres, especially of the 1700's. To begin with there is the St. Charles Theatre, commissioned by Charles of Bourbon as "the largest in Europe", built in just eight months by Antonio Medrano and inaugurated in 1737. Its 19th century façade, by Antonio Niccolini, consists of five arches surmounted by an elegant loggia. The interior of the San Carlo glitters with gold and

red, has 185 boxes in six tiers, a huge stage (140 square metres), a luxurious golden curtain supported by two winged victories around the royal box, and finally, on the vault, a painting of the 1800's by Giuseppe Cammarano. With its 3000 seats, the San Carlo has been for two centuries a centre for music lovers in Europe. After the success of Cimarosa and Paisiello, Bellini's first opera was performed here (The Sleep-walker), as well as Donizzetti's (Lucia di Lammermoor) and Rossini's (Moses); the latter composer moved then to Naples earning a particular renown in this splendid theatre. The theatre in the Royal Palace, called the "Small Court Theatre of the Bourbons", is of the same architectural value as St. Charles. It did not originate as a theatre, though, but as a reception hall; it became a theatre only in 1768, after Fuga's remodelling, when Paisiello himself inaugurated it, and it remained famous for a long time.

The Mercadante Theatre dates from 1778, nowadays with a 19th century façade, different than the original. It was preceded by the New Theatre (1724) by Mancino, whose work is said to have inspired the Teatro della Scala in Milan; in the New Theatre, Caruso began his legendary career. The 1800's saw the birth of the Bellini Theatre (1864), which witnessed the triumph of Bizet's Carmen. It also was the long-standing home of Scarpetta's theatre company, and of the Sannazzaro Theatre (1860), built by Fausto Niccolini, son of Antonio, recently the home of the Neapolitan Comic Theatre. The San Frediano Theatre is very famous and popular in Naples. It started as an opera house at the end of the 1700's and now is the permanent home of the great Eduardo De Filippo.

The Museums

The National Archaeological Museum

At the top of the Santa Teresa hill is the National Archaeological Museum. It probably has the world's richest collection of Greco-Roman art.

It also has precious specimens from the Stone, Bronze, and Iron ages, as well as an outstanding collection of ancient Egyptian art.

From the first half of the 1700's this beautiful Palace has sheltered various collections, from that of Charles of Bourbon, inherited from his mother Elisabeth Farnese, to the collections from ancient Rome (Caracalla, Palatino), to those objects found during excavations of Pompeii, Herculaneum and Stabia.

It is virtually impossible to list in its entirety the collection of wall-paintings, mosaics, sculptures, the golden, silver, marble and bronze objects, the coins, the numerous models, the armour, furnishings and everyday items.

It will suffice for the moment to mention the most outstanding works, to wit: on the ground-floor there is a huge Bust of Jupiter, the two famous youths called The Tyrannicides (a copy of a 6th century sculpture), the splendid statue of the Spearman (of wonderful proportions and deriving from Polycletus' original), the big Hellenistic statue of Flora, the Diana of Ephesus (in bronze and marble, of great technical and symbolical significance), the

Mosaic of Alexander, detail

world-renowned Farnese Bull (which comes from Caracalla).

The bronzes fill twenty rooms, followed by the Emperors' Gallery and a collection of portraits, among which Caesar, Augustus, Homer, and a splendid Horse's Head.

Equally rich is the first floor of the Museum, displaying mostly ancient paintings and mosaics that were recently excavated near here.

It is the most exhaustive collection of its kind. Exceptionally are the The Cock Fight, a Festoon with Fruit and the huge mosaic of the Battle of Alexander and Darius, originating from Pompeii, where the horses' movements are harmoniously connected to the perspective of the spears raised in battle. On the second floor of the Museum is the large Hellenistic group of the Farnese Atlas, the realistic Portrait of Proclus and his Wife, the Farnese Cup, an incomparable chisel-work on an enormous cameo.

Finally, there are innumerable golden and glass items, vases, bronzes and terracottas.

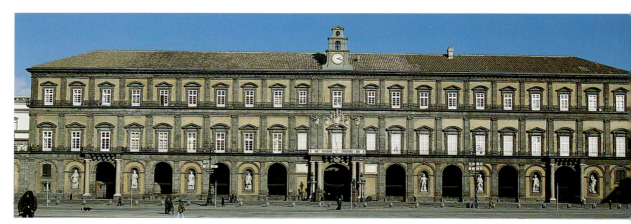

Royal Palace, façade

Royal Palace

After a hundred years of Spanish domination, a viceroy –the Count of Lemos– decided to build a suitable royal palace for a possible visit of Philip III, King of Spain. The construction of the Royal Palace, by Domenico Fontana, began in 1600 and was completed in 1650. Various changes were later made Vanvitelli in the mid-1700's. He eliminated, among other things, a few low arches in the façade in order to create the niches hosting the statues of the major kings of Naples: Roger the Norman, Frederic II, Charles I of Anjou, Alphonso I of Aragon, Charles V, Charles III of Bourbon, Murat, Victor Immanuel II. The façade is divided into three orders, marked by Doric, Ionic, and Corinthian pilaster strips. The marvellous Bronze Door by Guglielmo Monaco leads to the Honour Staircase, a work of Picchiatti. Worth visiting are the Chapel, the Teatrino di Corte (Small Court Theatre) (see the chapter on Naples' Theatres), and the sumptuous Royal Apartments, filled with neo-Baroque and late-empire furniture, stuccoes, paintings and period chandeliers. There is also the remarkable Throne Room with a Titian (Portrait of Luigi Farnese), the Oratory (the queen's private chapel), the Bedroom of the Queen with works of Baciccia, Corenzio, with a beautiful copy of Filippino Lippi's Madonna with Child and St. Joseph, the extended frescoed Hall of the Ambassadors.

In other halls there are various paintings, frescoes and tapestries by Zuccari, Guercino, Vaccaro and Codazzi.

Hall of the diplomats

The Palace also contains the important National Library of Naples, with over one and a half million volumes and a series of papyri found in Herculaneum and Pompeii. Finally, there are some autographed texts by Tasso, Leopardi, Gianbattista Vico.

 naples

Giovanni Bellini, Transfiguration

The National Gallery

Masaccio, Crucifixion

The big Farnese collection together with various later collections in forty five rooms, give an overview of Italian and European art. Every piece is of exceptional quality.

The Gallery opens with the 13th century Stories of St. Dominic and the truly splendid

St. Ludovic of Tolosa crowns Robert of Anjou by Simone Martini.

Besides some 14th century paintings by Masolino, we see the admirable Crucifixion by Masaccio (1426): it belonged to a polyptych preserved for a long time in the Church of the Carmine in Pisa, then taken apart and distributed in the 1700's; since 1901 it has been in the Capodimonte Museums. There are Renaissance works by Pinturicchio, Signorelli and Sandro Botticelli (Madonna with Child).

Later masterpieces are Bellini's beautiful Transfiguration, Titian's Portrait of Pope Paul III Farnese and Correggio's Gypsy Girl (actually a Madonna).

There are other beautiful paintings by Lorenzo Lotto, Mantegna, Parmigianino, the Carraccis, Guido Reni, Mattia Preti and Luca Giordano.

Our last visit after this tour of exceptional quality is to the rich private collections (paintings and objects) of the Nineteenth Century Gallery.

St. Martin's Museum

Around the mid-1800's in the splendid St. Martin Chartreuse on the Vomero, an important museum was organised. It should be visited by those genuinely eager to understand Naples and its history. The museum holds mainly records of the history of Naples. Besides the Orilia Collection (porcelains, glassware, snuff-boxes) and the naval section, the Neapolitan section includes a fundamental topographic collection (with the view by Iafrery of 1566 and the view by Stopendael of 1660), and various landscapes and other Neapolitan works from the 1700's and the 1800's (Gigante, Smargiassi, and others). The actual picture-gallery contains works by Caracciolo, Salvator Rosa, Micco Spadaro, the wonderful Self-portrait by Luca Giordano, and still-lives of the Posillipo school. The Manger Collection (mainly 18th century) is unique. The famous Cuciniello Manger, in particular, has very rare pieces. The Costume Collection and the Festivities Section are important for an understanding of Neapolitan culture. Finally, in the sculpture section, there are the works of the great Tino da Camaino, who worked in the 1300's on the building of the Monastery which was once where the Chartreuse is now.

Domenico Gargiulo, Revolt of Masaniello, St. Martin's Museum

The Filangieri Museum

The 15th century Cuomo Palace (a gift of king Alphonso of Aragon to the Cuomo family), often rearranged and finally purchased –around the middle of the 1800's– by Prince Gaetano Filangieri, houses the Filangieri Museum, and collects objects such as weapons, shields, medals, naval souvenirs, but also paintings of high value by Luca Giordano, Domenichino, Giuseppe Ribera, Federico Barocci. A rare and elegant hanging passage leads to an enormous Hall where one can admire glass showcases, ceramics and valuable portraits. The Library, of particular interest to scholars, contains excellent books on the history of Naples.

The Pignatelli Museum

The Pignatelli Museum is in the splendid Acton Villa, named after the English noble who built it in 1830. It was successively owned by Rotschild and by Diego Aragona Pignatelli Cortes, duke of Monteleone (end of the 1800's). The museum holds remarkable porcelain and 19th century furniture. There are also beautiful furniture, looking-glasses and elegant furnishings, with Vienna, Berlin, Meissen, Capodimonte, Venice and Doccia (Florence) porcelains. In the Dining Room there are luxurious table services and porcelains. There is the interesting Garden with rare exotic plants, where the beautiful Coach Museum stands.

Royal Palace and Museums of Capodimonte

On the hill of the same name are the beautiful Royal Palace and the Park. The Royal Palace was commissioned by Charles III of Bourbon (who originally intended to build a shooting-lodge) to the architect Antonio Medrano in 1743. In a wood of almost seven square kilometres, arranged later as a park with rare and exotic plants, the palace was built by Sanfelice, who built the vast radiating avenues within a splendid landscape-garden. In the park one should visit the Villa of the Princes, the famous Porcelain Factory by Sanfelice, the curious Chapel of San Gennaro (by the same builder, with a beautiful painting by Solimena), the Pheasantry, the Cottage of the Queen (built by Fuga) and the 19th century Capuchin Monastery. The whole is a most interesting mixture of architecture and landscape, and a favourite walk with the Neapolitans. The magnificent Royal Palace is made up of a succession of luxurious halls, culminating in the huge Reception Hall. There is the wonderful Porcelain Parlour, with precious rococo-style decorations by Fisher and Restile, built for Mary Amalia of Saxony. An absolute must see is the very precious collection of the Capodimonte Porcelains (its factory was later moved to Portici, starting a production in a very different style). Then there are the superb ceramics of the Ciccio collection, the tapestries, the prints, the musical instruments. The Capodimonte Royal Palace has a rectangular plan, with three courtyards, and is built on two levels bounded by a balustrade. At the end of the building are some extruding bodies; the façade shows a central portal subdivided into three. The whole building is marked by pilaster strips diminishing in dimension.

The National Ceramic Museum

In the pleasant Villa La Floridiana, built in neo-classic style by the architect Niccolini for the duchess of Floridia at the beginning of the 19th century, with its beautiful view over the Belvedere, is the National Ceramic Museum, of undoubted interest to collectors.
The pieces are from all ages and all parts of the world. There are articles from Capodimonte, Faenza, Savona, Deruta, Urbino, Venice, Meissen, Limoges, Malaga, Wedgwood, as well as a section of rare oriental ceramics on the lower level. Finally, there is a collection of cane-handles from the 18th century and one very rare example of a porcelain pitcher from the 16th century.

Other Museums

Naples is the city of music: San Pietro a Maiella has a Historic Museum of the Music Conservatory well worth a visit (if open). There are varied and interesting items such as portraits and souvenirs of great composers, Domenico Scarlatti's inkstand and Rossini's music-stand. Naples has also produced many scientists as the many Science Museums prove, among which the Anatomic Museum of Veterinary Science, Anthropology Museum (with specimens prior to Homo Sapiens from every part of the planet), Mineralogy Museum (with 30,000 items arranged in seven collections), Palaeontology Museum (50,000 fossil finds), Zoological Museum (founded by Murat, showing rare ornithological collections, sponges, mammoths, and the Bourbon collections), and the Zoological Station with Europe's oldest Aquarium.

Subterranean Naples

St. Gennaro's Catacombs

Naples is built over a subterranean town where seven hundred cavities and caves flank a path built from more than a million cubic metres of tuff (a material Neapolitans have dug up for millennia, using it to build everything, including the ancient town walls). The entrance to subterranean Naples is at the side of the Church of St. Paul Major in San Gaetano Square: from there it ramifies into a thick network of hypogea (underground cemeteries), aqueducts, tombs, tunnels, caves, and ossuaries. The Greeks were skilled underground builders: visit the Necropolis in via Nicotera with its exhibits from the 8th and the 7th centuries, and also the Hypogea (Cemeteries) of the Virgins, Crystals and the Sanatorium, with its walls decorated by stuccoes and paintings and with sarcophagi carved in the rock.

Around 50 AD the Romans built under Naples the Claudian Aqueduct, leaving us the Neapolitan Crypt, which-going through Posillipo hill-reaches the Flegreian Fields and the Seiano Cave at the base of the same hill. The Christians of the first centuries used this network for their clandestine meetings and to bury their followers and martyrs. Worth a visit are St. Gennaro's Catacombs dating from the 2nd century AD; from there the exit takes us into via Capodimonte. Even bishops are buried here, such as San Gennaro, before his relics were moved to the Cathedral.

The numerous frescoes are amongst the earliest paintings of San Gennaro, the Good Shepherd, Adam and Eve; there is the interesting marble stone, dedicated perhaps to the cult of Priapus, and a baptismal font of the 8th century.

Of great interest are also the catacombs of San Gaudioso. The nearby Cemetery of the small Fountains, very dear to the Neapolitans, is more recent. To the ancient underground excavations have been added nowadays subterranean works such as the Railway Galleries (the Cuman, the Circumflegreian Galleries) and the Funicular Galleries (Chiaia, Montesanto, Posillipo). Underground Naples, once the realm of clandestinity and persecutions, an air-raid shelter during World War Two, is today the cause of the precariousness of the very land on which Naples stands, vexed as it already is by recurrent landslides and floods.

naples

Vesuvius

Campagna is a volcanic region and amongst the numerous craters of the Flegreian Fields in the volcanic islands that surround the Gulf of Naples, Vesuvius dominates: a threat for millennia. Vesuvius, born of telluric formations twelve thousand years ago, is the only active volcano in continental Europe. Its outline and height have changed through the ages (it was once two thousand metres high, today it is two thousand two hundred seventy metres high). Since its last big eruption in 1944, it has lain dormant; the cloud of dust that was so characteristic of the Parthenopean landscape, has disappeared.

Vesuvius has been at once a blessing and a curse. In fact, if its periodic eruptions during the centuries (beginning with the terrible eruption of 79AD) have brought destruction and death to entire villages and towns, on the other hand they have fertilised the surrounding soil, producing a luxuriant vegetation. Historians and writers of ancient times (such as Diodoro Siculo, Vitruvius and Strabo) speak of the forests and vineyards that once were here. Following the dreadful earthquake of 63 AD, in 79 AD Pompeii and Herculaneum were tragically destroyed, as described in the famous letters by Pliny the Younger who had seen it from a distance. From a rift (two kilometres wide) in the mountain's side burst forth: sparks, hot mud, gas, lava, burning rocks and ashes. Since then, through the centuries, eruptions have followed one after the other, varying in force, without any regularity. There were the powerful eruptions of 472, 993, 1038, 1500, and finally of 1631, when ten successive lava streams destroyed a series of villages, causing over four thousand deaths. The eruption of 1906 was very powerful and left Vesuvius diminished in height by almost two hundred metres and altered in profile.

Today Vesuvius has two peaks of different dimension and shape facing respectively north and south. The whole volcanic body is fifty metres above sea-level and has a perimeter of about forty kilometres; the part of the volcano called Mount Somma is 1132 metres high, Vesuvius proper is 1270 metres high.

There are many popular excursions to this volcano; the easiest one starts from Resina (near Herculaneum), crosses the Plain of the Brooms, goes up the tuff-slopes of the Hill dei Canteroni where the Vesuvian Observatory is located and reaches the panoramic Humbert Hill, Margaret Hill, and finally the crater's edge.

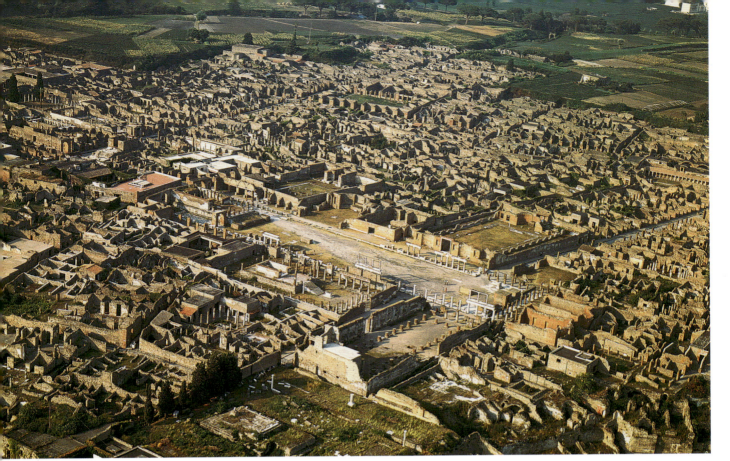

Pompeii

Pompeii has as yet been only partially excavated. It has an area of fifty hectares and is visited by tourists from all over the world. Before the 24th of August 79AD it was a blooming trading centre with a population of thirty thousand. "On the ninth day before September there is an enormous black cloud looming on the horizon" according to Pliny the Younger. A cloud of poisonous gases, ashes and incandescent lava buried those people trapped in town and suffocated others trying to escape towards the sea (as the petrified corpses found scattered all over Pompeii, witness to). Pompeii, as a wealthy town, had plenty of splendid public buildings and lavish residences; its inhabitants had fought against the Samnites and against the Romans, who finally turned it into a colony, though it retained a spirit of independence. It came under Greek (especially of the nearby Cuma), Etruscan and Samnite influence, so that its town-structure and its buildings fluctuate between Greek and Italic styles. The eruption of 79 buried it for many centuries, until in the 1700's the first excavations brought it to light. Excavation techniques were at first unscientific, but improved during the 19th century. Today, digs are bringing to light further finds; archaeologists are now much more concerned about the preservation of the finds.

Apart from throwing new light on an old town and its population, the excavations also make possible an insight into ancient Roman art (especially visual art). The wall paintings show at least four different ages and styles: "encrustation-painting" with the prevalence of reds and yellows; "architectural painting" where the walls are covered with images of architectural studies as in the famous Villa of the Mysteries; "Egyptian-style" painting with its very delicate wall decorations as in the "Cupid"–frieze in the Casa dei Vettii; and finally "architectural illusionism", displaying an almost Baroque abundance. Of great value are the mosaics: among the most significant is the Battle of Alexander in the House of Faunus. The numerous sculptures in marble, bronze and terracotta, under strong Hellenistic influence (some are intentional copies of Greek masterpieces), are valuable. Of special interest are Apollo and Diana in the Temple of Apollo, Apollo playing the Harp, the Ephebe from the house bearing this name, the Dancing Faun, and the Wild Boar assaulted by Hounds.

It would be difficult to single out any one exhibit during a visit to Pompeii. Memorable are: the Forum, Pompeii's political, religious and economic centre; the elegant Basilica and the Temple of Apollo, with almost all of its columns still in place; the severe Temple of Vespasian and the Temple of Jupiter; the Thermae of the Forum, the evocative Sepulchre Street, the splendid and sumptuous Villa of the Mysteries, containing one of the most significant pictorial cycles of antiquity. Because of its life-sized figures, this vast painting vividly depicts what could be the Dionysian Mysteries, an anonymous work of the 1st century BC; other interesting places are the Villa of the Cupids with its peaceful perystile, the perfectly preserved House of the Vettii, the Great Theatre and the Small Theatre.

By visiting Pompeii, we get an insight into everyday life here as it was with its shops, stalls and furnishings. It is as though a moment in time has been frozen and preserved for us through the centuries, leaving us to meditate on the vicissitudes of man.

Herculaneum

The Trellin-work House

After eighteen centuries of oblivion, Herculaneum, a small town at the foot of Vesuvius almost at the centre of the Gulf, is reappearing little by little as it is exhumed from the twelve metres of volcanic material under which it has been buried and, paradoxically, kept intact not only with regard to the walls, but also to the wooden jambs and the furnishings. The excavations were unofficially begun by an Austrian prince in 1709, but only officially in 1738. It brought to light the famous Villa of the Papyri, where old perfectly preserved papyri were found. Only in 1927 did the excavations start following a systematic program (still in progress).

There is so much to see here: the Trellis-work House, only extant example of a multi-family house with porch and loggia, the House of the Wooden Partition Wall, the Central Thermae with the small frigidarium for the cold baths, the large tepidarium and the calidarium; the House of Carbonised Furniture, the House of Neptune and Anafritis with its mosaic decorations, the Maximum Decuman, a very evocative main street in Herculaneum, the House of Telefus, the biggest and most luxurious house in the southern part of town. The House of Telefus gets its name from a small relief of neo-attic style, representing the myth of Telefus. The house contains a Hellenistic hall bounded by a porch and some large rooms decorated with exceptionally beautiful multicoloured marbles.

As in Pompeii, the tragedy and magic of this place speak to us through the ages.

Oplontis

Villa of Poppea, east wall

In the strict sense of the word, Oplontis, close by Pompeii and Herculaneum, was never a town. It was a residential area of sumptuous villas built in the splendid inlet, today called Torre Annunziata. Two buildings here are worth visiting: the Villa of Poppea (Nero's wife) and the Villa of Crassus. The first one has about a hundred rooms, an enormous swimming-pool and extraordinary wall paintings. Different is the Villa of Crassus, who was perhaps a wealthy farmer.

Less luxurious, it imitates the structure of an agricultural country house, and contains a curious exhibit: four hundred pitchers full of mould.

Sorrento

In the Sorrento peninsula that stretches into the Tyrrhenian Sea and divides the gulfs of Naples and Salerno, amongst pleasant villages such as Saiano and Sant'Agata, rises from the sea the lovely small Sorrento, renowned for over two thousand years. Good fortune has gathered here the best the world can offer: an incomparable landscape, a crystal clear sea, a climate that remains mild even in winter, traces of a splendid past (the Villa of Pollio Felice); the lively colourful to-and-fro – so typical of the Neapolitans – through lanes, alleys, boats and painted houses. Sorrento is heavenly to visit and even more so to live in. It was no idle whim that inspired poets, writers and musicians to sing the praises of this land in immortal pages; this land that gave birth to Torquato Tasso. Sorrento rises on a jutting rock perpendicular to the sea. Because of its fame it has given its name to the whole promontory. The urban plan is based on the old Roman camp, the cardo being the busy via Tasso and the decumano via Cesare. Piazza Tasso is the daily meeting-place of tourists and locals who mix happily together in Sorrento. In fact, the many open-air cafés, with panoramic views or in quaint little squares, contrast with the enchanting maze of steps and alleys, terraces that from the centre of the small town lead to an endless view of the sea. Sorrento is at once a place to explore or in which to remain in quiet contemplation, enjoying the warm breezes and the blue sea. Old and new, Roman and 18th century, vestiges of both are   dotted about Sorrento. It attracts many tourists from all over the world; in winter it is a refuge for those seeking a perfect climate, in summer it attracts those who enjoy swimming from elegant beaches in a sea that shines with a green reflected light. A tour of this charming little town can start either from Piazza Tasso, which has a monument to the poet, or from the nearby statue of St. Anthony Abbott, patron saint of Sorrento. The cathedral should be visited. Outside rises, on an old Roman arch, an elegant bell tower. The cathedral dates from 1000 AD, but it was rebuilt in the 15th century.

naples

Over the marble portal is the Aragon coat-of-arms. The church has three naves and is decorated with 14th century bas-reliefs and outstanding paintings of the 17th century. The choir covered in Sorrento marquetry is very beautiful. Another church to visit is San Francesco d'Assisi in Piazza Gargiulo. Do not miss the nearby cloister with its elegant mullioned windows, nor, quite near, the Villa Comunale. From its terrace can be had a unique view of the Gulf of Naples. The "Sedile Dominova" is an old 15th century loggia, the seat of the Sorrento aristocracy. Inside there are coats-of-arms and 18th century paintings. Every walk in Sorrento will inevitably lead, sooner or later, either to the Marina Grande or to the Marina Piccola. The former has bathing establishments, the latter an enchanting little port. Into the distance stretches a crystal clear sea; behind there is a magnificent picture of olive trees, lemon and orange groves, a vision that unites the sky, the earth and the sea. An outstanding monument in Sorrento is Palazzo Correale of Terranova with an interesting museum adjoining it. The palace is 18th century and houses a valuable art collection, the gift of Alfredo Correale, Count of Terranova. Amongst the most beautiful objects are Greek and Roman vases and lovely furniture from the 17th and 18th centuries, of various origin. The china collection is splendid, containing pieces created by the famous local manufactory of Capodimonte, besides Sèvres and Chinese. The book lover can admire rare old volumes in the library, notably the Jerusalem Delivered by Tasso. Finally, from the belvedere of the palace, framed between rich orange and lemon groves, the lady in all her immortal beauty, the sea.

The Islands of Naples

Capri, view of Faraglioni

Capri

Six kilometres long, about two wide, ten square kilometres in area, Capri has been for two thousand years a dream-island, or perhaps better the dream of an island. The Romans, particularly Tiberius, selected it because of the beauty of its landscape, the climate, the transparent waters. Today artists and thinkers such as August von Plate, Gorki, Ada Negri, Axel Munthe and Curzio Malaparte, have chosen the island either for their holidays or as their home.

The island, with a population of thirteen thousand, in addition to the tourists, can be reached from the Great Marina harbour; from here you climb to the heart of Capri, the "piazzetta" (small square). It has rightly been called "the heart of the world" (a few square metres where people stop to talk, to have a drink, as in a living room, where the whole planet is gathered); from here one climbs the famous eight hundred steps and reaches Anacapri.

Besides the climate, the sea and the landscape, which one can enjoy in every part of this green and cool island, there is a variety of things to be seen. For the antique-lovers there are the Baths of Tiberius, embedded in the rocks, or the superb Villa Jovis, which was the glamorous villa of the emperor himself. Large and well preserved, it is located on a cliff high over the sea. It has an area of seven thousand square metres, has a tank system for the water supply and many baths, and a variety of drawing rooms, reception rooms and bedrooms. A splendid loggia of a hundred metres long puts a finishing touch to it all; unfortunately its frescoed walls were mostly destroyed. You really should not miss the San Costanzo Church (10th century), the white Santo Stefano Church (17th century), and especially the Chartreuse of St. James, a great monastery with the Small and the Large Cloisters, the annexed Convent (today a school and library), and finally the Clock Tower.

There are also the Gardens of Augustus, a very large park full of plants and flowers of every kind, and Krupp Street, a lovely path that goes from the gardens to the sea from which, at every curve, spectacular views can be enjoyed.

The Piazzetta

naples

Blue Grotto

Small Marina is a well-equipped seaside resort that offers every convenience, but above all unbelievably limpid seawater and a safe mooring point for pleasure boats. The unforgettable rendezvous of the island, though, is the Grotta Azzurra (Blue Grotto). It is a natural cave, thirty metres high and fifty five by fifteen.

You must stoop in your boat to pass the extremely narrow entrance, but once through it, you will be surprised by the magical view: light comes from under the water (in fact the opening through which it filters is under the sea) and lends to the water itself and to the rocky walls a gentle blue colouring, almost surreal.

A leap in time and we go from here (rediscovered after two thousand years only at the beginning of the 19th century) to the modern St. Michael's Villa, built by the writer Axel Munthe, a Swedish physician, author of a very well known book, dedicated to Capri: "The History of St. Michael". It has a beautiful bower, the Gallery of Statues and a small but well stocked Museum with a renowned Sphinx, which supposedly brings good luck to who-ever touches it.

We are now in Anacapri, first a Phoenician, then a Greek settlement; it is today the second centre of the island. From its heart, Vittorio Square, we approach St. Michael Church, a work of the 18th century by Vaccaro, and the gorgeous St. Sophia Church with its white and dynamic façade.

Our first and last vision is the famous Faraglioni. Three huge solitary rocks in close proximity rise from the sea to a height of almost a hundred metres. Faraglioni, crowded by flocks of seagulls, can be visited by boat. It is a breathtaking sight to the approaching visitor. From a distance it looks like a curious, natural coat-of-arms for this peerless island.

Ischia

The harbour

Ischia is the largest of the three islands in front of Naples (46 kilometres of surface, 37,000 inhabitants); the beauty of this place is legendary, and it is an international tourist centre. An ancient Greek settlement, it retains traces of later ages, as for example the wonderful Castle, a witness of the Aragonese rule. The clear sea reflects the harmony of the coast, the green of the pine-forests and of the renowned vineyards.

The centre of the island is formed by two places called Porto and Ponte. Ponte resembles an 18th century village, with its fishing houses, fish market, and peaceful little shops, but also has ancient and noble churches such as Santa Maria della Scala and Santo Spirito.

In Porto, where there are magnificent and luxurious hotels, boats and hydrofoils can land. The most famous spas are Casamicciola and above all Lacco Ameno. Famous foreigners have stayed here, such as the fairytale writer Andersen, the musician Mendelssohn, the scientist Madame Curie; nowadays tourists seek cures from the thermal and mud baths. The Sanctuary of Santa Restituta (11th century) is remarkable and most probably the oldest building on the island. A local attraction is the so called Fungo (Mushroom), a small tuff rock in the shape of a mushroom rising from the sea, possible result of an old eruption of lava.

Forio, a small, delightful village, is characterised by its eight towers, especially by the Torrione (the keep), a 15th century building, once a watchtower, later a prison. Near the central Church of St. Mary of Loreto, in Baroque style, is the picturesque, blinding white Chiesa del Soccorso, which has a variety of styles, from the Renaissance to the Baroque. Finally, among the vineyards, there is the beautiful Sanctuary of Santa Maria del Monte (St. Mary's Mount), where annually on the 8th of May a pilgrimage takes place.

The most picturesque point of Ischia is perhaps Sant'Angelo, with its small harbour, its tiny pink houses, its nets and fishing boats, and with that curious protuberance called Sant'Angelo Point. Every view is beautiful. It is also extraordinarily peaceful as mules are the only form of transport here. Places to stop at are the Gardens of Aphrodite and Apollonius. Adventurous visitors can try to reach the open-air Cavascura Springs, remarkable for their extremely hot water.

naples

ITALIAN CUISINE

Cappelletti Soup
Serves 8

Puff pastry, 500 g
Lean Veal: 80 g
Lean Pork: 80 g
Chicken breast, 50 g
Ham, 80 g
Parmesan cheese
Breadcrumbs, 50 g
1 Egg
1 Nutmeg
1 Clove
Butter, 80 g
Beef and capon stock, about 2 lt
Salt and pepper

Preparation

Brown the meat in the butter with the clove
and mince them in a food processor along
with the ham.
Return the meat mixture to a pan along
with the Parmesan cheese, breadcrumbs, egg,
some nutmeg, salt and pepper.
Mix thoroughly until smooth.
Roll out the puff pastry and cut it into 3 cm squares.
Put some filling on each square and fold the
squares diagonally to make triangles,
sticking the opposite corners together.
Bring the broth to a boil and cook the cappelletti
in it. Serve very hot with grated Parmesan cheese.

Italian cuisine

Amatriciana Spaghetti

Serves 4

Bucatini or spaghetti, 350 g
Ripe small tomatoes or canned, 350 g
Lean bacon or pancetta, 100 g
Grated Roman Pecorino cheese
Chilli pepper
Olive oil
Salt and pepper

Preparation
Brown the diced
bacon in a frying pan
with four tablespoons
of olive oil and
then add the small
tomatoes. Add salt,
pepper and some
chilli pepper.
Let it cook for
about ten minutes over
high heat.
Cook the bucatini
or spaghetti in
boiling water,
strain it firm
and mix with
the tomato sauce.
Serve with
extra grated
pecorino cheese.

Penne all'arrabbiata

Serves 4

Penne 500 g
Porcini mushrooms, 300 g
Lean bacon, 150 g
Tomatoes, 500 g
Garlic
Basil
Chilli pepper
Grated Parmesan cheese
Olive Oil »

Preparation
Dice the mushrooms and cook them in olive oil and bacon for about 20 minutes. Add the chilli pepper, the mashed tomatoes, basil, garlic and cook for a few minutes.
Cook the penne in plenty of boiling water, strain them firm and serve with the sauce and grated Parmesan cheese.

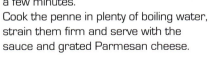
Italian cuisine

Rice with Squills

Serves 4

Rice 300 g
Squills 500 g
4 garlic cloves
White wine
Parsley
Olive oil
Salt and pepper

Preparation

Wash the squills and boil them for about 20 minutes in a litre of quite salty water with two garlic cloves and a glass of white wine. Let them cool in their broth and then cut them lengthways; mince the squill lean finely.

In another pan brown the garlic cloves with parsley in 6 tablespoons of olive oil and add the squills lean.

Cook for about 5-6 minutes and then add the rice and the remaining squill broth. Some minutes before serving sprinkle the rice with parsley.

Serve very hot with pepper.

Spaghetti and Crabs
Serves 4

Thin Spaghetti or linguine, 400 g
Crabs, 500 g
Peeled tomatoes, 500 g
2 garlic cloves
White wine
Extra-virgin olive oil
Parsley
Chilli pepper
Salt

Preparation

Break and cut the crabs in big pieces. Place 7 tablespoons of olive oil in a pan and brown the garlic, parsley, chilli pepper and then add the crabs and two glasses of white wine.

Add salt and cook over low heat for about a quarter of an hour.

Add the tomatoes and let it cook for half an hour stirring well.

Remove the crabs from the sauce, peel them and put them back into the sauce. Heat the sauce and add more parsley.

Cook the thin spaghetti firm and sauté them with the sauce.

« Viareggina Cacciucco
Serves 6

Soup fish: 600 g
Dogfish 500 g
Cuttlefish 800 g
Prawns 300 g
Squills 400 g
Mussels 500 g
4 garlic cloves
Parsley
Chilli pepper
Fresh ripe tomatoes or canned 600 g
Red wine
Bread
Olive oil
Salt and pepper »

Preparation

Clean, scale and cut the fish into pieces, the molluscs and the shellfish.

Take a deep pan and brown 3 garlic cloves with finely minced parsley and chilli pepper in half a glass of olive oil.

As soon as the garlic turns golden add half a glass of red wine and let it evaporate, then add the chopped tomatoes, salt and after 5 minutes add the chopped cuttlefish.

Cook for 20-25 minutes and then add the squills and the fish.

Cook for extra 15-20 minutes (do not stir or the pieces of fish will break) with some broth if necessary.

Now add the prawns and the mussels and let it cook for 15 minutes.

In the meantime prepare some slices of garlic bread and line them in a big bowl, cover them with the hot and thin cacciucco.

Ladle the cacciucco over the slices of bread in the bowl, so as it is quite dry and serve.

Stuffed Squids
Serves 4

Squids 1 Kg.
2 anchovy fillets
30 g salted capers
1 garlic clove
Parsley
Breadcrumbs or the soft part of a loaf
1 egg
1/2 glass of white wine
Olive oil
Salt and pepper »

Preparation

Clean the squids, cut the squid tubes from the heads and remove the intestines, wash them in cold water.

Push out the beak and eyes. Wash the heads and mince them with garlic, anchovies, capers and parsley. Place the mixture in a bowl and stir it with the egg adding 2 tablespoons of olive oil, 2 tablespoons of breadcrumbs (or the soft part of a loaf), a tablespoon of vinegar, salt and pepper.

Stuff the squid tubes with this mixture and fasten the squids with toothpicks.

Place the squids in a baking dish, pour some white wine over them, 8 tablespoons of olive oil, salt, pepper and bake over medium heat for about 20-25 minutes.

 Stewed Prawns

Serves 4

12 prawns
Parsley
Chilli pepper
3 garlic cloves
White wine
Olive oil
Salt

Preparation
Wash the prawns and slit them open.
In a saucepan heat 8 tablespoons of olive oil, minced garlic, parsley, and chilli pepper until garlic turns golden.
Add the prawns and brown them over low heat on both sides.
Add salt and half a glass of white wine and let it evaporate.
Serve very hot and sprinkle with minced parsley.

Italian cuisine

Ribollita
Serves 6

Stale bread, 300 g
1 black cabbage
Dried white beans, 400 g (soaked overnight)
1/2 Savoy cabbage
2 potatoes
2 carrots
3 bunches Swiss chard
2 onions
2 stalks celery
1 tablespoon tomato sauce
Salt and pepper
Olive oil

Preparation
Place the beans in 2 litres of cold water,
boil them and sauté ¾ of the purée in the
bean cooking liquid. Brown a chopped onion
in 8 tablespoons of olive oil and then add the
tomato sauce with hot water or broth,
sliced carrots and celery, Swiss chard and
thick sliced potatoes.
Add salt and pepper, cook for a few minutes
with the lid on and then pour all the bean cooking
liquid in the pan.
Cook long and when all the vegetables
are well soft add the slices of bread
and the remaining beans.
Boil for 10 minutes, stir and let it cool. Pour the
soup in a bowl and sprinkle with finely chopped
onion, pepper and a little oil.
Bake until the onion turns golden.

Italian cuisine

Pizza "Bella Napoli"

ingredients for the dough

- Flour, 400 g
- Active dry yeast, 20 g
- Water
- Salt
- Extra-virgin olive oil

Preparation

Soft the yeast in little water, add two bunches of flour, stir well and let the dough rise for about half an hour in a slightly floured bowled. Place the leavened dough in the middle of the remaining flour and knead it adding a pinch of salt, until smooth and elastic. Roll the dough out in your favourite shape. Top it and pour little olive oil on. Bake in a very hot 220 degree oven.

Ingredients for the topping

Tomato sauce, Buffalo mozzarella cheese from Campania, Pachino tomatoes, black olives, capers, basil.

Arugola Focaccia

ingredients for the dough

Flour, 400 g
Active dry yeast, 20 g
Water
Salt
Extra-virgin olive oil

Preparation

Soft the yeast in little water, add two bunches of flour, stir well and let the dough rise for about half an hour in a slightly floured bowled. Place the leavened dough in the middle of the remaining flour and knead it adding a pinch of salt, until smooth and elastic. Roll the dough out in your favourite shape. Top it and pour little olive oil on. Bake in a very hot 220 degree oven.

Ingredients for the topping

Arugola, fresh tomatoes, Buffalo mozzarella cheese from Campania, Valtellina bresaola (dried soft beef) and lemon.

© Copyright 2006
Ats Italia Editrice S.r.l. – Rome
Editrice Giusti S.r.l. – Florence
Kina Italia/EuroGrafica S.p.A. – Italy

GRAPHICS PROJECT, PAGING AND COVER: Sabrina Moroni – Roberta Belli (Ats Italia Editrice)
SCANNING AND CHROMATIC CORRECTIONS: Ats Italia Editrice (Leandro Ricci) – Kina Italia/EuroGrafica
CARTOGRAPHY: L.A.C. – Florence
PRINTING: Kina Italia/EuroGrafica – Italy
PHOTOGRAPHY:
Archivio Ats Italia Editrice – Rome
(Bocchieri, Borra, Buonafede, Busi-Guerrini, Cirilli, Cozzi, Giordano, Grassi, Regoli, Tini)
Archivio Editrice Giusti – Florence
(Cellai, Griffoni, Leoni, Mazzola)
Archivio fotografico SCALA – Florence
Archivio Kina Italia/EuroGrafica – Italy
Foto Musei Vaticani – Reverenda Fabbrica di San Pietro

The publishers are at the disposal of all holders of copyright photographs not identified.

DISTRIBUTION:
Ats Italia Editrice – 00163 Rome – via di Brava, 41- 43 – tel. 0666415961
Editrice Giusti – 50141 Florence – l.go Liverani, 12-13 – tel. 0554220577
Kina Italia/EuroGrafica – 36035 Marano Vic.no – via del Progresso, 125 – tel. 0445698745

Questo volume è disponibile anche in lingua italiana
Ce volume est disponible aussi en français
Dieser Band ist auch in deutscher Sprache erhältlich
Esta obra también está publicada en español
Este volume está disponível também em língua portuguesa
Данное издание опубликовано также на русском языке
Nimniejsza książka dostępna jest też w języku chińskim
此书并有中文版
本書には日本語版もあります
이 바타리 안내책자는 한국어로도 출판되어 있습니다